English

Assessment Papers

8–9 years

Great Clarendon Street, Oxford, OX2 6DP, United Kingdom

Oxford University Press is a department of the University of Oxford. It furthers the University's objective of excellence in research, scholarship,and education by publishing worldwide. Oxford is a registered trade mark of Oxford University Press in the UK and in certain other countries

British Library Cataloguing in Publication Data
Data available

978-0-19-277990-8

10 9 8 7 6

Printed in China

Acknowledgements

The publishers would like to thank the following for permissions to use copyright material:

Illustrations: Nigel Kitching, K Kett and Beverly Curl
Page make-up: OKS Prepress, India
Cover illustrations: Lo Cole

Pp5–6 extract from *A House Called Awful End* by Philip Ardagh, copyright © 2002, published by Scholastic Ltd. Reprinted with permission by Faber and Faber Ltd and Henry Holt; p18 extract from *The Seven Voyages of Sinbad the Sailor* by John Yeoman, copyright © 2003, Chrysalis Children's Books; pp21–22 extract from *Blitz* © The Estate of Robert Westall 1994 reproduced by permission of Laura Cecil Literary Agency; p25 'Zanzibar' from *Walking on Air* by Berlie Doherty © 1993 Hodder Children's Books, reproduced by permission of David Higham Associates; p30 'Stopping by Woods on a Snowy Evening' from *The Poetry of Robert Frost* edited by Edward Connery Latham, published by Jonathan Cape. Reproduced by permission of the Random House Group Ltd; p36 extract from *Traitor* by Pete Johnson, published by Corgi Yearling. Reprinted by permission of the Random House Group Ltd; p39 extract from *The Copper Treasure* by Melvin Burgess published by A&C Black; pp45–46 extract from *Beaver Towers* by Nigel Hinton © 1995 Nigel Hinton. Reprinted by permission of Penguin Books Ltd; p52 'Billy Doesn't Like School Really' by Paul Cookson. Reproduced with permission of the author; pp55–56 'Ghost soup' from Kingfisher Treasury of Spooky Stories. Copyright © Kingfisher Publications Plc. Reproduced by permission of the publisher, all rights reserved.

Although we have made every effort to trace and contact all copyright holders before publication this has not been possible in all cases. If notified, the publisher will rectify any errors or omissions at the earliest opportunity.

Links to third party websites are provided by Oxford in good faith and for information only. Oxford disclaims any responsibility for the materials contained in any third party website referenced in this work.

The manufacturer's authorised representative in the EU for product safety is Oxford University Press España S.A. of El Parque Empresarial San Fernando de Henares, Avenida de Castilla, 2 – 28830 Madrid (www.oup.es/en or product.safety@oup.com). OUP España S.A. also acts as importer into Spain of products made by the manufacturer.

Before you get started

What is Bond?

This book is part of the Bond Assessment Papers series for English, which provides **thorough and continuous practice of key English skills** from ages five to thirteen. Bond's English resources are ideal preparation for many different kinds of test and exam – from SATs to 11+ and other secondary school selection exams.

What does this book cover?

It practises comprehension, spelling, grammar, punctuation and vocabulary work appropriate for children of this age. It is fully in line with the National Curriculum for English and the National Literacy Strategy. One of the key features of Bond Assessment Papers is that each one practises **a wide variety of skills and question types** so that children are always challenged to think – and don't get bored repeating the same question type again and again. We think that variety is the key to effective learning. It helps children 'think on their feet' and cope with the unexpected.

The age given on the cover is for guidance only. As the papers are designed to be reasonably challenging for the age group, any one child may naturally find him or herself working above or below the stated age. The important thing is that children are always encouraged by their performance. Working at the right level is the key to this.

What does the book contain?

- **20 papers** – each one contains 40 questions.

- **Scoring devices** – there are score boxes in the margins and a Progress Chart on page 68. The chart is a visual and motivating way for children to see how they are doing. Encouraging them to colour in the chart as they go along and to try to beat their last score can be highly effective!

- **Next Steps** – advice on what to do after finishing the papers can be found on the inside back cover.

- **Answers** – located in an easily-removed central pull-out section.

- **Key English words** – on page 1 you will find a glossary of special key words that are used in the papers. These are highlighted in bold each time that they appear. These words are now used in the English curriculum and children are expected to know them at this age.

How can you use this book?

One of the great strengths of Bond Assessment Papers is their flexibility. They can be used at home, school and by tutors to:

- provide regular English practice in **bite-sized chunks**

- **highlight strengths and weaknesses** in the core skills

- identify **individual needs**

- set **homework**

- set **timed formal practice** tests – allow about 30 minutes.

It is best to start at the beginning and work though the papers in order.

What does a score mean and how can it be improved?

If children colour in the Progress Chart at the back, this will give an idea of how they are doing. The Next Steps inside the back cover will help you to decide what to do next to help a child progress. We suggest that it is always valuable to go over any wrong answers with children.

Don't forget the website…!

Visit www.bond11plus.co.uk for lots of advice, information and suggestions on everything to do with Bond and helping children to do their best.

Key words

adjectival phrase	a group of words describing a noun
adjective	a word that describes someone or something
adverb	a word that gives extra meaning to a verb
adverbial phrase	a word or phrase that makes the meaning of a verb, adjective or another adverb more specific, for example The Cheshire cat vanished quite slowly beginning with the end of its tail.
alphabetical order	the order found in the alphabet
antonym	a word with a meaning opposite to another word *hot – cold*
collective noun	a word referring to a group *swarm*
compound word	a word made up of two other words *football*
conjunction	a word used to link sentences, phrases and words *and*, *but*
consonant letters	all letters of the alphabet apart from a, e, i, o, u (vowel letters)
contraction	two words shortened into one with an apostrophe placed where the letter/s have been dropped *do not = don't*
definition	the meaning of a word
diminutive	a word implying smallness *booklet*
fronted adverbial	an adverbial that has been moved before the verb, for example The day after tomorrow I'm going on holiday.
homonym	a word that has the same spelling as another word, but a different meaning turn *left*, we *left* the room
homophone	a word that has the same sound as another, but a different meaning or spelling *right / write*
noun	a word for someone or something
past tense	form of a verb showing something that has already happened
personal pronoun	a pronoun used when writing about ourselves or others *I, you, he*
phrase	a group of words that act as a unit
plural	more than one *cats*
prefix	a group of letters added to the beginning of a word *un, dis*
present tense	form of a verb showing something happening now
pronoun	a word often replacing a noun
proper noun	the name of a person, place etc. *Ben*
root word	a word to which prefixes or suffixes can be added to make other words *quickly*
singular	one *cat*
suffix	a group of letters added to the end of a word *ly, ful*
syllables	the beats in a word
synonym	a word with a very similar meaning to another word *quick – fast*
verb	a 'doing' or 'being' word
vowel letters	the letters a, e, i, o, u

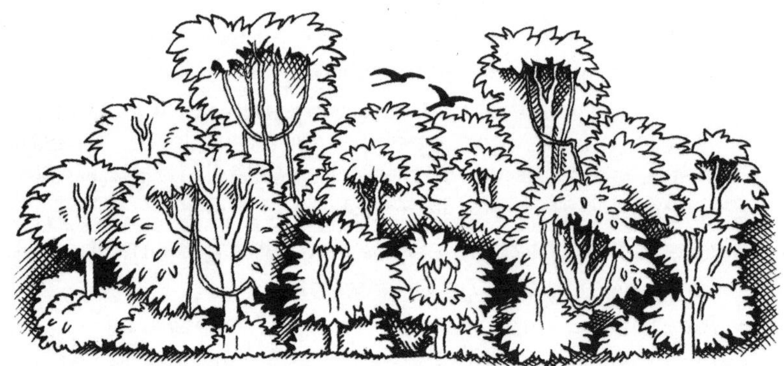

Rainforests

Tropical rainforests provide the richest habitat on Earth for living things. They only cover 11 per cent of the planet's land surface but contain over half its plant and animal species. Rainforests are found around the Equator, in regions with a hot temperature all the year round and heavy daily rainfall. The rainforests are found in South America, Central Africa, South Asia and the Pacific islands.

The rainforest grows in a series of layers, reaching up to the light. Trees can grow to heights of 25–45 metres. Their tops form the canopy, which acts as a ceiling for the whole forest. It shields the forest against soil erosion from heavy rain. Some individual trees grow above the canopy to form an emergent layer. The further down the forest you go, the darker it gets. Only 2 per cent of sunlight actually reaches the ground because of the thick vegetation higher up.

Each layer supports its own special range of species. The canopy provides a home for brightly coloured birds, such as toucans and macaws, and a few mammals, such as sloths and monkeys. The layer below is called the understory. Birds, butterflies, snakes and frogs inhabit this layer. Between the understory and the forest floor, lies the shrub layer. This is made up of ferns and small shrubs. The forest floor itself is the place where all the dead plants and leaves rot down to make the soil that keeps the forest alive. The larger animals live here: leopards and gorillas in Africa, tigers and elephants in Asia, tapirs and jaguars in South America.

The rainforest is very fragile. It depends on the thin layer of soil for its food. If the trees are cut down, the soil quickly becomes barren and unable to support plant life again. It reverts to desert. At present the rainforests are being destroyed at an alarming rate for timber. Perhaps 50 rainforest species are becoming extinct every day. The tribal people who live in the forests are being displaced. Forest destruction is one cause of the warming of the whole planet.

Underline the right answers.

1 Which of these continents does not contain rainforests?

(Asia, Africa, Europe, South America)

2 Which of these species live in the understory?

(macaws, sloths, butterflies, monkeys)

3 The rainforest is being cut down for (space, timber, light)

Answer these questions.

4 How does the canopy protect the rainforest?

____

5 Write these layers of the rainforest in order, topmost one first:

shrub layer, emergent layer, understory, forest floor, canopy.

(1) _______________   (2) _______________   (3) _______________

(4) _______________   (5) _______________

6 What does 'fragile' in line 23 mean?

____

7 What does 'displaced' in line 28 mean?

____

8–9 Give two reasons why cutting down trees in the rainforest is damaging.

____

____

Underline a **noun** in each line.

10 pretty   book   went   she   busy

11 it   large   ready   new   desk

12 brown   Wednesday   ran   some   our

13 legs   dirty   them   broken   their

14 interesting   house   long   dull   her

15 from   Hannah   get   old   tipped

16 paper   badly   sad   come   too

Spell these words correctly. Each word has missing vowels.

17 y____ ____ng

18 c____ ____ntry

19 tr____ ____bl____

20 t____ ____ch

21 d____ ____bl____

5

Add a sequence word at the beginning of each sentence so that it makes sense.

While   After   Then   First

22–25 ____________ Tina sat in her chair while her teacher took the

register. ____________ she copied some sentences from the board.

____________ her teacher collected in the homework, Tina was writing.

____________ she had finished copying the sentences she was allowed

out to play.

4

Circle the words that have two **syllables**.

26–31

fall   bellow   arrow   eel

puppet   sparrow   wobble

pill   tree   pillow

6

Rewrite the short passage, putting in the missing capital letters and full-stops.

32–40 mr scott visited edinburgh and glasgow each friday then he travelled on the overnight train to london

____

____

____

9

When Eddie Dickens was eleven years old, both his parents caught some awful disease that made them turn yellow, go a bit crinkly around the edges, and smell of old hot-water bottles.

There were lots of diseases like that in those days. Perhaps it had something to do with all that thick fog, those knobbly cobbled streets and the fact that everyone went everywhere by horse … even to the bathroom. Who knows?

'It's very contagious,' said his father.

'And catching,' said his mother, sucking on an ice cube shaped like a famous general.

They were in Eddie's parents' bedroom, which was very dark and dingy and had no furniture in it except for a large double bed, an even larger wardrobe, and thirty-two different types of chair designed to make you sit up straight even if your wrists were handcuffed to your ankles.

'Why are you sucking an ice cube shaped like a famous general?' Eddie asked his parents, who were propped up against piles of pillows in their impressively ugly double bed.

'Doctor Muffin says that it helps with the swelling,' said his mother. In fact, because she had a famous-general-shaped ice cube in her mouth, what she actually said was, 'Dotter Muffin schez va it hewlpz wiva schwelln,' but Eddie managed to translate.

'What swelling?' he asked politely.

His mother shrugged, then suddenly looked even more yellow and even more crinkly round the edges.

'And why do they have to be famous-general-shaped?' asked Eddie. He always asked lots of questions and whenever he asked lots of questions his father would say: 'Questions! Questions!'

'Questions! Questions!' said his father.

Told you.

'But why a famous general?' Eddie repeated. 'Surely the shape of the   *30*
ice cube can't make any difference?'

'Schows sow muck chew no,' muttered his mother, which meant (and
still means), 'Shows how much you know.'

His father rustled the bedclothes. 'One does not question the good
doctor,' he said. 'Especially when one is a child.' He was a small man   *35*
except for when he was sitting up in bed. In this position, he looked
extremely tall.

Then Eddie's mother rustled the bedclothes. It was easy to make them
rustle because they were made entirely from brown paper bags glued
together with those extra strips of gummed paper you sometimes get if   *40*
you buy more than one stamp at the post office.

Postage stamps were a pretty new idea back then, and everyone
– except for a great-great-great-aunt on my mother's side of the family
– was excited about them.

From A House Called Awful End by Philip Ardagh

Underline the right answers.

   1 Why did Eddie think there were lots of diseases 'in those days'?

     (because it was cold, because people did not eat enough, because it was foggy)

   2 Eddie's parents' bedroom had (no, a little, lots of) furniture in it.

   3 Why had Doctor Muffin recommended chewing ice cubes?

     (because they were cool, because they were easy to make, because they helped with a swelling)

Answer these questions.

   4 What happened to Eddie's parents when he was eleven?

____

   5 What does 'contagious' mean in line 8?

____

   6 Why was it easy to rustle the bedclothes?

____

   7–8 List two details from the story that show that it was set a long time ago.

____

____

9 Say in your own words why you think this is going to be a rather strange story.

____

Underline the two **antonyms** in each line.

    10 right   back   left   correct

    11 dark   light   day   winter

    12 young   happy   dirty   clean

    13 funny   rich   poor   ill

    14 danger   safety   crash   freedom

    15 here   now   then   where

Add the missing commas to these sentences.

    16 Diane is making a blouse a skirt and a dress.

17–18 Steven bought some potatoes carrots cabbages and onions.

19–21 At school we study English mathematics history geography and art.

Add the **suffix** _ness_ or _ment_ to each of these words.

    22 weak__________   **23** agree__________

    24 pay__________   **25** enjoy__________

    26 blind__________   **27** state__________

    28 quiet__________   **29** ill__________

Underline an **adjective** that best describes the word in bold.

    30 station   three   pink   heavy   busy

    31 pencil   wet   sharp   sleepy   hot

    32 hands   ten   happy   clean   first

    33 June   sunny   foggy   dark   frosty

    34 hair   sticky   sweet   quiet   straight

Match each word with its meaning. Write the number next to the word.

35 carrot	______	(1)	a funny picture
36 carpet	______	(2)	he makes things out of wood
37 carton	______	(3)	a vegetable
38 cartoon	______	(4)	a cardboard box
39 carol	______	(5)	floor covering
40 carpenter	______	(6)	a song

6

Now go to the Progress Chart to record your score!   Total   **40**

Paper 3

Scene 1

Mr Williams' classroom
Writing on blackboard – 'Mr Williams
is a silly old fool'

Mark and Andy are playing in Mr Williams' classroom during playtime.
They should have been outside. Suddenly they hear footsteps coming
down the corridor.

Mark   Quick! Hide! He is coming, I can hear his footsteps.
Andy   Where? He has eyes in the back of his head. Even if we
            hide he will know we are here.
Mark   We must try – what about the store cupboard?

They both rush over to the store cupboard.

Footsteps getting closer.

Mark   It's locked.
Andy   Hurry up! Under Mr Williams' table.

Mark and Andy sitting under table.

Mark   I wish I hadn't written anything on the blackboard!

Sound of two sets of footsteps coming into the room.

Andy	*(whispering and peering under the desk)* It's not Mr Williams, it's a woman. I can see the legs. I think it's Mrs Wilkinson. She wears those shoes with the flat buckles. And there's someone else there. It looks like Miss Jones – black trousers, blue shoes with laces.
Mrs Wilkinson	*(to Miss Jones)* Now we're alone, Caroline, we can discuss the matter. *(suddenly catches sight of the board and laughs.)* He is too. Should have retired years ago, silly old fool. We'd better wipe it off though ... Anyway, as I was saying, what happened?
Miss Jones	Well, I left my handbag in the staff room and when I went back to look for it, the Head was coming out, very quickly, holding a large supermarket bag.
Mrs Wilkinson	Well, Caroline? So what?
Miss Jones	When I looked in the staff room, my handbag was gone.

Underline the right answers.

1 Which scene of the play is this?

(Scene 1, Scene 2, don't know)

2 Where did the boys first want to hide?

(behind a desk, under the teacher's table, in the store cupboard)

3 Miss Jones wore (flat shoes with a buckle, blue shoes with laces, trainers)

Answer these questions.

4 Why couldn't the boys hide in the cupboard?

____

5 What was Miss Jones's first name?

____

6 What made Mrs Wilkinson laugh?

____

7 What was Miss Jones suggesting the Head might have done?

____

8–9 What do you think happens next?

____

____

Circle the words that are spelt correctly.

10–13
        enough   quater

    exersise   naughty

    oposite   importent

    interest   striaght   promise

Name the **collective noun** for each of the following.

14 twelve cows _______________

15 a large number of wasps _______________

16 a large area of trees _______________

17 a handful of flowers _______________

18 a group of sheep _______________

19 a side of football players _______________

Arrange these words in the order you would find them in the dictionary.

    colour   dark   eel   dragon   egg   change

20 (1) _______   **21** (2) _______   **22** (3) _______

23 (4) _______   **24** (5) _______   **25** (6) _______

Underline the fronted adverbial in each of these sentences.

26 Before we leave, make sure you have been to the toilet.

27 The day after tomorrow, I'm going to Australia

28 Later that morning. I heard the school had flooded.

Write three sentences that begin with a fronted adverbial.

29 ____

30 ____

31 ____

Rewrite the **proper nouns** with capital letters.

swamp   birmingham   prince william   dexter

august   chester   block   monday   tap

abigail   mrs jones   magician   thursday

32 _______________   33 _______________   34 _______________

35 _______________   36 _______________   37 _______________

38 _______________   39 _______________   40 _______________   9

Now go to the Progress Chart to record your score!   Total   40

Strange, strange, is the little old man
Who lives in the Grange.
Old, old, and they say that he keeps
A box full of gold.
Bowed, bowed, is his thin little back   5
Which once was so proud.
Soft, soft, are his steps as he climbs
The stairs to the loft.
Black, black, is the old shuttered house.
Does he sleep on a sack?   10
They say he does magic, that he can cast spells,
That he prowls round the garden listening for bells;
That he watches for strangers, hates every soul,
And peers with his dark eye through the keyhole.
I wonder, I wonder, as I lie in my bed,   15
Whether he sleeps with his hat on his head?
Is he really a magician with altar of stone
Or a lonely old gentleman left on his own?

Underline the right answers.

    1 The man is (small, tall, medium height).

    2 People say he keeps (jewels, gold, silver, pennies) in a box.

    3 He walks upstairs (quietly, quickly, noisily).

Answer these questions.

    4 What do people say he can do?

____

    5 What do people say he listens for?

____

6 What is a 'loft'?

____

7–8 Write two words that describe the man.

____________   ____________

9 If the man is not a magician, what could he be?

____

Add the correct **homophone** in each sentence.

10 hear or **here** I can __________ the train coming.

11 write or **right** Sam got all the answers __________.

12 stares or **stairs** Grandpa climbed the __________ one at a time.

13 saw or **sore** Kate __________ the horse galloping.

14 road or **rowed** Tuhil and Frank __________ as fast as they could.

15 Witch or **Which** __________ cake shall I have?

Underline the words that are spoken in these sentences.

16 "Quick, come here!" yelled the teacher.

17 "I'm waiting for my tea," answered Greg.

18 The children muttered, "Wish we didn't have to go to bed!"

19 "Shh, the baby is asleep," whispered Dad.

20 "You do look silly!" laughed Rupa.

Rewrite these sentences, making the **plurals singular**.

21 The trees swayed in the wind.

____

22–23 The boys ate the sweets.

____

24 The barking dogs scared the girl.

____

25–27 Sophie collected the ponies and led them to the buckets of food.

____

Make eight **compound words** out of the eleven short words.

card   worm   butter   man   cup   ball

snow   earth   post   egg   board

28 _______________   **29** _______________

30 _______________   **31** _______________

32 _______________   **33** _______________

34 _______________   **35** _______________

Write *am*, *is* or *are* in the sentence so that it makes sense.

36 They _______________ going to the beach.

37 I _______________ really going to miss you.

38 We _______________ going to have a ride tomorrow.

39 David _______________ very upset.

40 The twins _______________ sharing a bedroom.

Now go to the Progress Chart to record your score!   Total   40

BIGVILLE WEEKLY ECHO

Homes facing the bulldozer

by Mike Smeaton

Heartbroken council tenants in the Nanton area of Bigville have little to celebrate over Christmas. They have just been told that their houses could be demolished because the council does not have the money to repair them.

The council recently surveyed 80 Westway type houses and found they were in very poor condition. They have severe structural problems and the repair bill has been put at 4.8 million.

Westway houses have steel frames and were built in large numbers to meet Britain's population growth in the 1950s. The houses were prefabricated in sections in the factory and bolted together on site. It was a quick and cheap solution to Britain's housing problem after the war. For speed, chemicals were used to harden the concrete. It was found in the 1980s that when exposed to water, the chemicals rotted the steel. Repairs were done in the 1990s to slow down the decay, but now the council thinks the damage is beyond repair. 'We simply don't have the funds to repair the houses any more,' said John Kennaway, the council engineer. 'Anyway it would be a very difficult task.'

Local residents are confused and angry. 'Quite honestly, it's made for a terrible Christmas,' said Jane Adams, who has lived in Ringway Close for 51 years. 'Many of us have lived here all our lives. I love my home and it's not just buildings that we're talking about. A whole community could be destroyed.'

Mrs Adams, who chairs the Residents' Association, said that the money should be found to preserve the houses. The council says it simply does not have the cash. Jeff Johnston, the councillor for housing, said there was no easy solution. Part of the problem is that the houses are semi-detached and some of them have been sold to private owners. If it wanted to bulldoze them, the council would have to buy back the privately owned houses first.

Underline the right answers.

1 Westway houses were built (before the war, during the war, after the war).

2 What is Jeff Johnston's job?

(councillor for housing, chair of the Residents' Association, council engineer)

3 Westway homes are (detached, bungalows, semi-detached).

Answer these questions.

4 What reason is given for Britain's housing problem after the war?

____

5 Why were chemicals useful in building Westway houses?

____

6 What does 'prefabricated' in line 19 mean?

____

7 Write two words to describe how local residents feel about the problem.

(1) _________________________   (2) _________________________

8 Why doesn't Jane Adams want the houses destroyed?

____

9–10 Give two reasons why the council cannot repair the houses.

(1) ____

(2) ____

11 Explain in your own words what Mrs Adams meant when she said 'A whole community could be destroyed' (lines 42–43).

____

Spell each of these words correctly.

12 vien

13 thay

14 nieghbour

15 wiegh

16 obay

17 eghty-eight

Circle the **pronouns** in each sentence.

18–19 They thought he sang beautifully.

20–21 It was the best day he could remember.

22–23 He said she was very clever.

24–25 They screamed to make him hear.

Underline the **root word** in each of these words.

26 dislike   **27** jumping   **28** unkind

29 frighten   **30** passed   **31** altogether

Rewrite these two sentences, adding the missing punctuation and capital letters.

32–36 david was unsure what day it was was it thursday

Underline a **synonym** for the word in bold.

37 pointed	shiny	sharp	dull	sloping
38 circle	square	peg	round	oblong
39 nation	country	ribbon	food	strip
40 busy	lazy	hard	soft	active

Now go to the Progress Chart to record your score!   Total   40

My father, who was a very rich merchant, died when I was
still a child, leaving me enormous wealth and property and
land. When I became a young man and could get my hands on
the money, I spent and spent on expensive clothes and fine living,
treating all my friends to the very best of everything – as if the money   5
would last forever. But finally I came to my senses and realised that if I
carried on in this way I should soon be facing poverty.

So I resolved to do something about it. I sold my remaining
possessions and fine clothes for three thousand dirhams, enough to fund
me for a journey to foreign parts. And with the money I bought some   10
goods to trade with and all I needed for a long voyage, and joined a
company of merchants on board a vessel bound for Basra, where we
changed ship. We sailed for weeks on end, travelling through the Persian
Gulf and into the Arabian Sea, going from island to island, until finally we
reached an island that looked just like the gardens of Paradise.   15

We cast anchor and landed, and in no time we were busying ourselves
in our different ways: making ovens in the sand, cooking, washing,
exploring, and playing games to amuse ourselves. At one point I thought
I felt a small earth tremor, but nobody else seemed to notice it. They just
carried on with what they were doing. I went off with a small group to   20
explore, but we hadn't ventured very far before we heard the ship's
captain hailing us from the gunwale at the top of his voice.

'Run for your lives!' he was calling. 'Drop everything and get back on
board. This isn't an island, after all. We've landed on a monstrous fish
that's been asleep so long that the sands have settled over it and the   25
trees have sprung up on it. But when you lit your fires it felt the heat and
began to stir. At any moment it will plunge down into the depths, taking
you all with it. Get back to the ship before you drown!'

We didn't need any persuading, I can tell you. We abandoned our
bundles of merchandise, our spare clothes, our cooking pots, and   30
everything else in our mad scramble back to the ship.

From *The Seven Voyages of Sinbad the Sailor* by John Yeoman

Underline the right answers.

1 The father of the person in the story had been a (sailor, merchant, soldier, fisherman).

2 Which of these seas did the ship sail to?

(the Indian Ocean, the Black Sea, the Arabian Sea, the Pacific Ocean, the Persian Gulf)

3 The fish woke up because of (an earth tremor, the shouting of the men, the fires).

Answer these questions.

4 Say in your own words why the person in the story needed to change his life.

____

5 What does 'resolved' mean in line 8?

____

6 Why did the passengers and crew not notice they had landed on a fish?

____

7 What warning did the person telling the story have that there was something strange about the island?

____

8 How do you think the people felt when they discovered that they weren't on an island?

____

Add the **prefix** or **suffix** *al* to each of these words.

9 _____ways_____   10 _____historic_____   11 _____so_____

12 _____ready_____   13 _____mechanic_____   14 _____medic_____

15 _____accident_____   16 _____though_____   17 _____most_____

Write each of these verbs in the **past tense**.

18 walk _______________   19 jump _______________

20 pull _______________   21 sprint _______________

22 push _______________   23 listen _______________

Put one of the **conjunctions** in each of the spaces below.

until   but   because   so

24 Marianne stayed at home _______________ she had a cold.

25 The sea is quite warm _______________ we can go swimming.

26 Mum is going out now _______________ she will be back soon.

27 'Don't eat the biscuit _______________ you've finished your lunch.'

28 We will stay here _______________ dad asked us to.

Write the *nch* or *tch* word to match each picture.

29

l_______________

30

i_______________

31

s_______________

32

b_______________

33

p_______________

34

s_______________

Using a line, match each word with its correct **definition**.

35 voyage   every year
36 remedy   a long journey
37 summit   a piece broken off something
38 annual   a large, deep spoon
39 ladle   a cure
40 fragment   the top

Rosie hurried on. The pubs were further apart now and even the alleys were silent. Just the odd moggie, poor things, scavenging at the pigswill bins.

She was just bending down to stroke one when the siren went. For the third time that day. Rosie got the usual sinking feeling in her gut, but she wasn't all that worried. Air-raid sirens couldn't kill you. She listened intently, through the dying drone of the siren, for the sound of bombers' engines…

And heard nothing.

She'd carry on for a bit, try and get home before anything happened. Her ma would worry if she was caught out in a raid. Ma might even leave the shelter and come looking for her, as far as the chippie in Scobie Street. Then batter Rosie over the ear when she found her, for causing so much worry.

'G'night, moggie. Best of British Luck!'

Her footsteps quickened; the gas mask banged harder against her bottom, as if urging her on.

She'd gone nearly half a mile before she heard the bombers coming. She was in a district she hardly knew. Really poor people, to judge from the state of their doors and windows. But you couldn't be choosy when the bombers came. You just ran for the nearest brick street-shelter with its concrete-slab roof.

Not many shelters round here. Poor people were always the worst looked after. Bet the toffs had shelters, and to spare, up Croxteth way …

She ran and ran. Turned a corner by a chapel with bombed-out windows. Saw the three brass balls of a pawnbroker's… Then a great square shelter loomed up.

She made the doorway, just as the first guns opened up overhead, turning the night white-black, white-black. Making a noise like some daft kid banging a tin tray right in your ear that echoed across the whole sky after.

Then she heard the shrapnel shrieking down like dead rockets on
Bonfire Night. And ducked through the blackout curtain into the shelter.

There was room by the door, on the slatted benches… She flung
herself into it, to get her breath back…

Still panting, she looked around.

And sighed. It seemed a totally miserable sort of shelter.

People huddled together in a dim blue light. Silent except for the
racking cough and the dismal wail of a baby at the far end.

35

From Blitz by Robert Westall

Underline the right answers.

1 What was Rosie doing when the siren went?

(looking for shelter, looking in pigswill bins, stroking a moggie)

2 She was carrying (a suitcase, a gas mask, an umbrella).

3 The guns sounded like (dead rockets, a tray being banged, the sea
hitting cliffs).

Answer these questions.

4 How did Rosie feel when she heard the sirens?

____

5 Why did Rosie think that her mother might hit her round the head?

____

6 How could Rosie tell that she had come to a poor area?

____

7 Who do you think the 'toffs' are in line 24?

____

8 Describe in your own words what made the shelter seem so miserable.

____

Put these words in the **past tense**.

9 go __________   **10** sing __________

11 jump __________   **12** fight __________

13 buy __________   **14** come __________

Rewrite these sentences using a more interesting phrase than the words in bold.

15 We had a good time at the **party**.

___

16 My **teacher** is very grumpy.

___

17 Daniel climbed out of the **pool** and got dressed.

___

18 The **baby** screamed until it was picked up.

___

19 The **children** had a fun day.

___

20 Joseph was reading a **book**.

___

Add the ly suffix to each of these words.

21 grumpy ___________   **22** poor ___________

23 sad ___________   **24** quick ___________

25 kind ___________   **26** happy ___________

27 stupid ___________   **28** rough ___________

Many railway lines link London with other parts of the country. There are two main lines to Scotland: one goes up the east side of the country through York and Newcastle, and the other goes up the west side, passing through Crewe and Carlisle. If you are travelling to North Wales you leave the main line at Crewe. There are fast trains from Liverpool, Manchester and Sheffield to London and it is much easier to travel from north to south than it is to travel from east to west. There is a fast service from London to the West Country which passes through Salisbury and Exeter. There is an excellent electric service between London and south-east England.

Underline the right answers.

29–30 Which two of these towns would you pass through if you were travelling from London to Scotland on the east side of the country? (Crewe, York, Salisbury, Manchester, Carlisle, Newcastle)

31 Which direction is it easier to travel in? (east to west, north to south)

Answer these questions.

32 If you were travelling to North Wales, where do you leave the main line?

____

33–34 Name two cities that have fast trains to London.

_______________   _______________

35 What is the service like between London and south-east England?

____

Add the missing commas to these sentences where a short pause or pauses are needed.

36–37 Harry a very nervous boy hated the thunderstorm.

38 The boys set off along the track anxious to get to the next village before dark.

39 Najib ran as fast as he could barely taking a breath.

40 Leena was starving having not had anything to eat all day.

Paper 8

Zanzibar

Zanzibar used to make me think
Of marzipan and stripes.
It has the sounds of bees in it, and zizz.

I didn't know it would smell of spice
of lemon grass and strips of cinnamon   5
green balls of pepper,

buds of cloves,
nutmeg and vanilla pods
and rain, and steamy rain.

Children cling beneath banana leaves   10
and splash home, laughing, through the mud.
Soon the rain will wash their homes away.

Their mothers watch the sky.
When the sun dries the earth
They will squat and scoop and daub   15
and build their huts again.

Zanzibar. Palm trees and red skies
Blue fireflies in the night
Cinnamon, cloves, and lemon grass, and rain.

by Berlie Doherty

Underline the right answers.

1 Zanzibar is (a colour, a smell, a sound, a place).

2 Which of these smells does the poet not mention?

   (vanilla, cinnamon, nutmeg, ginger, cloves)

3 At night in the poem you can see (stars, fireflies, the moon, the sea).

Answer these questions.

4 Find something that is green in the poem and something that is red.

____

5 What is the weather like in Zanzibar?

____

6 Why do the mothers need to watch the skies in Zanzibar?

____

7 Why might the sound of the word 'Zanzibar' remind the author of the sound of bees?

____

8 Do you think that the poet has been to Zanzibar? Use evidence from the poem to support your answer.

____

Write the missing **noun** with an apostrophe to show something belongs to someone.

9 The rabbit belonged to Dimitri. It was ________________ rabbit.

10 The crayons belonged to Jane. They were ________________ crayons.

11 The jacket belonged to Helen. It was ________________ jacket.

12 The bone belonged to Mop the dog. It was ________________ bone.

13 The rat belonged to Rajeeh. It was ________________ rat.

14 The books belonged to Soraya. They were ________________ books.

Write each of these words correctly. A letter in each word needs to be changed to a y.

15 mith ________   **16** gim ________

17 Egipt ________   **18** mistery ________

19 piramid ________

Circle the **nouns** that don't have a different **plural** form.

20–23   reindeer   gate   grapefruit   jacket

goldfish   fork   sheep   button

Underline a **synonym** for the word in bold.

24 aid	act	hinder	help	stop
25 drop	rain	prod	bounce	fall
26 sad	strict	unhappy	glad	ugly
27 quick	loud	fast	slow	quiet
28 several	few	both	some	none
29 enjoy	hate	like	suffer	drive
30 modern	new	old	ancient	great
31 depart	post	leave	come	send

Write the **plural** of each of these **nouns** ending in *f*.

32 hoof _______________   **33** shelf _______________

34 loaf _______________   **35** calf _______________

36 leaf _______________   **37** wolf _______________

Write an interesting sentence about each of the following.

38 your home

____

39 your hair

____

40 your teacher

____

Paper 9

How to make a Christmas pudding

You need:

1 cup plain flour

1 tablespoon mixed spice

$\frac{2}{3}$ cup brown sugar

3 cups mixed dried fruit

A pinch of salt

1 cup shredded suet

1 large egg, beaten

$\frac{1}{2}$ cup brown ale

Butter or margarine to grease the basin

1 Get a large mixing bowl. Mix everything in the bowl except the egg and the ale.
2 Add the egg and the ale. Stir them in. Put the mixture in a cool place and cover with a cloth. Leave for a day.
3 Grease a 900 ml/1.5 pint pudding basin. Cut out a circle of non-stick baking paper and line the bottom of the basin.
4 Stir the pudding again and tip it into the basin. Cover with a circle of greaseproof paper. Put an old saucer over the top. Then cover it with a double thickness of foil. Fold it over the edge of the basin all the way round. Tie string round to hold it on tight over the basin.
5 Put the basin into a steamer over a pan of boiling water. Cover with a lid. Steam the pudding for 6 hours. **Caution: you must check the steamer every half an hour to make sure there is enough boiling water in the pan. Top it up as needed.**
6 Re-cover the pudding. Store it in a cool place. Steam it for another 2.5 hours before serving it. Happy Christmas!

Write true or false by each of these statements.

1 You must have brandy to go in the pudding. __________

2 You put the butter or margarine into the mixture. __________

3 You need a rolling pin to make the pudding. __________

4 You need to beat the egg before you put it in. __________

5 You need to line the basin before you pour the mixture in. __________

6 Putting a string round the pudding basin helps to carry it. __________

7 You can make a Christmas pudding in a day. __________

Answer this question.

8 What do you think will happen if you do not check the steamer every half an hour while the pudding is cooking?

____

Write a more powerful **verb** for each of the verbs in bold.

9 Harry **walked** to Gary's house. _______________________________

10 "May I have a cake?" **said** Meena. _______________________________

11 Dave **took** his pen back from Ann. _______________________________

12 "Please can I watch television?" **said** Nigel. _______________________________

13 The man **ran** round the park. _______________________________

Put these words correctly into the table.

chef   echo

character

machine

scheme   brochure

14–19

words with...	
ch sounding 'sh' as in shout	**ch sounding 'c' as in cat**

The following sentences are not in the right order. Read them through carefully, and then write the numbers to show their correct order.

20 _____ (1) The cyclist lay on the road.

21 _____ (2) Then the policeman called for an ambulance.

22 _____ (3) A cyclist was knocked off his bicycle.

23 _____ (4) Finally the cyclist was taken to hospital.

24 _____ (5) Meanwhile a policeman arrived.

25 _____ (6) Next the ambulance arrived.

With a line, join each word with its **diminutive** (word implying smallness).

26 owl		duckling
27 cat		piglet
28 goose		owlet
29 pig		bullock
30 duck		kitten
31 bull		gosling

Rewrite the sentences, adding in the missing punctuation and capital letters.

32–35 the plane landed at heathrow airport a little late

____

36–40 tessa and claire admitted they were lost what were they going to do

____

Paper 10

Stopping by Woods on a Snowy Evening

Whose woods these are I think I know.
His house is in the village, though;
He will not see me stopping here
To watch his woods fill up with snow.

My little horse must think it queer   5
To stop without a farmhouse near
Between the woods and frozen lake
The darkest evening of the year.

He gives his harness bells a shake
To ask if there is some mistake.   10
The only other sound's the sweep
Of easy wind and downy flake.

The woods are lovely, dark, and deep,
But I have promises to keep,
And miles to go before I sleep,   15
And miles to go before I sleep.

by Robert Frost

Underline the right answers.

1 At what time of day is this poem set?

(morning, afternoon, evening)

2 Where does the owner of the woods live?

(in a farmhouse, in the woods, in a village)

3 Where does the rider stop his horse?

(in the woods, beside the woods, a long way from the woods)

Answer these questions.

4–5 Describe two sounds the rider can hear.

(1) ____

(2) ____

6 Why would the rider's horse think it 'queer' to stop where they have?

____

7 Which line in the poem tells you that the rider loves the woods, rather than is frightened of them?

____

8 How do you think you would feel about the woods if you were making the same journey? Why?

____

Write the word or words each of these **contractions** is made from.

9 should've ________________   **10** won't ________________

11 I'll ________________   **12** can't ________________

13 they've ________________   **14** isn't ________________

15 wouldn't ________________   **16** haven't ________________

Add the missing speech marks to these sentences.

17 Have you found the dog? asked Jim.

18 Let's go and play in the park, suggested Aman.

19 I don't think you have washed your face! joked Dad.

20 Are you enjoying the pizza? asked the waitress.

21 I wish it would stop raining, sighed Amy.

22 Where do you think you are going? asked Mrs Thrower.

Rewrite the word adding the **suffix** *ible* or *able*. (Remember, if the last letter of the word is a vowel, the last letter is usually dropped before adding the suffix.)

23 suit _______________

24 reason _______________

25 sense _______________

26 believe _______________

27 wash _______________

28 response _______________

Underline the **adverbs** in these sentences.

29 The old man shouted angrily at the children.

30 The child ran noisily along the corridor.

31 The cat slowly stretched her leg.

32 Billy neatly wrote the date at the top of the page.

33 The robin sang sweetly as the snow fell.

34 My Dad snored loudly in front of the television.

With a line, match a word in each column to make a **compound word**. Write the compound words.

over	room	**35** _______________
moon	fall	**36** _______________
some	head	**37** _______________
water	light	**38** _______________
drain	where	**39** _______________
class	pipe	**40** _______________

1 **Europe** (lines 5–6)
2 **butterflies** (line 17)
3 **timber** (line 26)
4 *It shields the forest against soil erosion from heavy rain.* (lines 9–10)
5 **(1) emergent layer, (2) canopy, (3) understory, (4) shrub layer, (5) forest floor** (lines 8–20)
6 *easily broken, delicate*
7 *moved on*
8–9 Two of the following: *the soil becomes barren / goes back to desert; species become extinct; tribal people are displaced; it helps to cause global warming.*
10–16 Refer to definition of noun in key words on page 1.
10 **book**
11 **desk**
12 **Wednesday**
13 **legs**
14 **house**
15 **Hannah**
16 **paper**
17–21 These words contain the short *u* sound spelt 'ou'. There is no particular rule for these words.
17 **young**
18 **country**
19 **trouble**
20 **touch**
21 **double**
22 **First**
23 **Then**
24 **While**
25 **After**
26–31 Refer to definition of syllables in key words on page 1.
   bellow, arrow, puppet, sparrow, wobble, pillow
32–40 Capital letters should be used for proper nouns (refer to definition of proper noun in key words on page 1) or at the start of a sentence. Mr Scott visited Edinburgh and Glasgow each Friday. Then he travelled on the overnight train to London.

Paper 2 (pages 5–8)

1 **because it was foggy** (line 5)
2 **lots of** (lines 12–13)
3 **because they helped with a swelling** (line 18)
4 *They caught an awful disease, turned yellow, went crinkly round the edges, smelled of old hot-water bottles.* (lines 2–3)
5 *Easy to catch / highly infectious*
6 *They were made out of brown paper bags.* (line 39)

7–8 Any two of the following: *the thick fog, the cobbled streets, everyone used horses, postage stamps were a new idea* (lines 5–6 and 42)
9 Answers should mention the nonsense elements in the story: *everyone went to the bathroom on horses, the famous general-shaped ice cubes, the large number of pieces of furniture in the bedroom, the bedclothes made out of brown paper bags.*
10–15 Refer to definition of antonym in key words on page 1.
10 **right, left**
11 **dark, light**
12 **dirty, clean**
13 **rich, poor**
14 **danger, safety**
15 **now, then**
16–21 Commas are used to separate items in a list. There is a comma between each item except for the final two, which are separated by 'and' instead.
16 Diane is making a blouse, a skirt and a dress.
17–18 Steven bought some potatoes, carrots, cabbages and onions.
19–21 At school we study English, mathematics, history, geography and art.
22–29 Refer to definition of suffix in key words on page 1. If a suffix starts with a consonant letter, it is added straight on to most root words without any change to the last letter of those words. There are some exceptions: the word 'argument'; and root words ending in '-y' with a consonant before it, but only if the root word has more than one syllable.
22 **weakness**
23 **agreement**
24 **payment**
25 **enjoyment**
26 **blindness**
27 **statement**
28 **quietness**
29 **illness**
30–34 Refer to definition of adjective in key words on page 1.
30 **busy**
31 **sharp**
32 **clean**
33 **sunny**
34 **straight**
35 carrot – **(3)** a vegetable
36 carpet **(5)** floor covering
37 carton – **(4)** a cardboard box
38 cartoon – **(1)** a funny picture
39 carol – **(6)** a song
40 carpenter – **(2)** he makes things out of wood

Paper 3 (pages 8–11)

1 **Scene 1**
2 **in the store cupboard** (Mark's 2nd speech and 2nd stage direction)
3 **blue shoes with laces** (Andy's 3rd speech)
4 **It was locked.** (Mark's 3rd speech)
5 **Caroline** (Mrs Wilkinson's 1st speech)
6 *The writing on the board because she agreed with it.* (2nd stage direction during Mrs Wilkinson's 1st speech)
7 *She was suggesting that the Head had stolen her bag.* (Miss Jones' speeches)
8–9 Child's own interpretation of what might happen next
10–13 **enough, naughty, interest, promise**
14–19 Refer to definition of collective noun in key words on page 1.
14 **herd**
15 **swarm**
16 **forest / wood**
17 **bunch**
18 **flock**
19 **team**
20 **change**
21 **colour**
22 **dark**
23 **dragon**
24 **eel**
25 **egg**
26–28 Refer to definition of fronted adverbial in key words on page 1.
26 <u>Before we leave</u>, make sure you have been to the toilet.
27 <u>The day after tomorrow</u>, I'm going to Australia.
28 <u>Later that morning</u>, I heard the school had flooded.
29–31 Child's own examples of fronted adverbials written into sentences.
32–40 Refer to definition of proper noun in key words on page 1.
Birmingham, Prince William, Dexter, August, Chester, Monday, Abigail, Mrs Jones, Thursday

Paper 4 (pages 12–14)

1 **small** ('little', line 1)
2 **gold** (line 4)
3 **quietly** ('soft', line 7)
4 *He can do magic, cast spells.* (line 11)
5 *He listens for bells.* (line 12)
6 *It is the room at the top of the house.*
7–8 Any two of: *old, strange, little, thin, lonely, bowed* (line 1, 5, 18)
9 *a lonely old gentleman* (line 18)

10–15 Refer to definition of homophone in key words on page 1.
10 I can **hear** the train coming. One way to remember which homophone to use in this case is to note the word 'ear' included in 'hear'.
11 Sam got all the answers **right**.
12 Grandpa climbed the **stairs** one at a time.
13 Kate **saw** the horse galloping.
14 Tuhil and Frank **rowed** as fast as they could.
15 **Which** cake shall I have.
16–20 Speech is surrounded by inverted commas (also known as speech marks). There must also be punctuation before the closing inverted comma.
16 "<u>Quick, come here!</u>" yelled the teacher.
17 "<u>I'm waiting for my tea,</u>" answered Greg.
18 The children muttered, "<u>Wish we didn't have to go to bed!</u>"
19 "<u>Shh, the baby is asleep,</u>" whispered Dad.
20 "<u>You do look silly!</u>" laughed Rupa.
21–27 Refer to definitions of plural and singular in key words on page 1. Most singular nouns can be made plural by adding an 's', therefore removing the 's' from a plural will leave its singular form. Nouns ending in 'y' can be made plural by changing the 'y' to 'ies', so these words should have the 'ies' replaced with a 'y' to make it singular.
21 The **tree** swayed in the wind.
22–23 The **boy** ate the sweet.
24 The barking **dog** scared the girl.
25–27 Sophie collected the **pony** and led **it** to the **bucket** of food.
28–35 Refer to definition of compound word in key words on page 1.
Any eight from the following: *cardboard, earthworm, buttercup, postman, snowball, postcard, eggcup, cupboard, snowboard, snowman*
36–40 The verb 'am' is always paired with the pronoun 'I'; 'is' is paired with singular nouns; 'are' is paired with plural nouns.
36 They **are** going to the beach.
37 I **am** really going to miss you.
38 We **are** going to have a ride tomorrow.
39 David **is** very upset.
40 The twins **are** sharing a bedroom.

Paper 5 (pages 15–17)

1 **after the war** (lines 21–23)
2 **councillor for housing** (lines 48–49)
3 **semi-detached** (lines 51–52)
4 **The population grew.** (line 18)
5 *They helped to harden concrete quickly; helped the houses to be made more quickly.* (lines 23–25)

6 *Made in advance.*

7 Two from: *heartbroken, confused, angry, upset.* (lines 35–36)

8 *Many residents have lived there all their lives. She loves her home. It would destroy the whole community.* (lines 39–43)

9–10 *It does not have the money; It does not own all the houses. / The houses are semi-detached and some are privately owned.* (lines 8–9, 52–53)

11 *Mrs Adams meant that if the houses were torn down, then the people who lived in them would have to move and the friendships they'd built would be destroyed.*

12–17 These words contain the *ay* sound spelt 'ei', 'ey' and 'eigh'.

12 **vein**
13 **they**
14 **neighbour**
15 **weigh**
16 **obey**
17 **eighty-eight**

18–25 Refer to definition of pronoun in key words on page 1.

18–19 **They, he**
20–21 **It, he**
22–23 **He, she**
24–25 **They, him**

26–31 Refer to definition of root word in key words on page 1.

26 **dis<u>like</u>**
27 **<u>jump</u>ing**
28 **un<u>kind</u>**
29 **<u>frighten</u>**
30 **<u>pass</u>ed**
31 **<u>altogether</u>**

32–36 Refer to Paper 1 Q32–40.
David was unsure what day it was. Was it Thursday?

37–40 Refer to definition of synonym in key words on page 1.

37 **sharp**
38 **round**
39 **country**
40 **active**

Paper 6 (pages 18–20)

1 **merchant** (line 1)
2 **the Arabian Sea** (line 14)
3 **the fires** (lines 26–27)
4 *He was spending all his money and he realised he would soon be very poor.* (lines 5–7)
5 *decided, determined*
6 *The fish was asleep; it was covered in trees and sand.* (lines 24–26)
7 *He felt a small earth tremor.* (lines 18–19)

8 *Surprised, frightened*

9–17 Refer to definitions of prefix and suffix in key words on page 1. Not many nouns end in '-al', but many adjectives do.

9 **always**
10 **historical**
11 **also**
12 **already**
13 **mechanical**
14 **medical**
15 **accidental**
16 **although**
17 **almost**

18–22 Refer to definition of past tense in key words on page 1. If the verb ends in two consonant letters (the same or different), the '-ed' suffix is simply added on to convert it to past tense.

18 **walked**
19 **jumped**
20 **pulled**
21 **sprinted**
22 **pushed**
23 **listened**

24–28 Refer to definition of conjunction in key words on page 1.

24 Marianne stayed at home **because** she had a cold.
25 The sea is quite warm **so** we can go swimming.
26 Mum is going out now **but** she will be back soon.
27 'Don't eat the biscuit **until** you've finished your lunch.'
28 We will stay here **because** dad asked us to.

29–34 The *ch* sound is usually spelt 'tch' if it comes straight after a single vowel letter.

29 **lunch**
30 **itch**
31 **stitch**
32 **bench**
33 **pinch**
34 **stretch**

35–40 Refer to definition of definition in key words on page 1.

35 **voyage – a long journey**
36 **remedy – a cure**
37 **summit – the top**
38 **annual – every year**
39 **ladle – a large, deep spoon**
40 **fragment – a piece broken off something**

Paper 7 (pages 21–24)

1 **stroking a moggie** (lines 2–4)
2 **a gas mask** (line 16)
3 **a tray being banged** (lines 29–30)

4 *She got a sinking feeling but she wasn't too worried.* (lines 5–6)

5 *Because she would be cross that Rosie had made her worry by being outside in a raid.* (lines 11–14)

6 *The state of the doors and windows; few shelters.* (lines 19–24)

7 *rich people*

8 *The light was dim; everyone was quiet because they were afraid; the noises of the person coughing and the crying baby were the only sounds* (lines 37–38)

9–14 Refer to definition of past tense in key words on page 1. Most of these are irregular, meaning that children will just need to learn them.

9 **went**

10 **sang**

11 **jumped** Refer to Paper 6 Q18–23.

12 **fought**

13 **bought**

14 **came**

15 *wild and noisy party*

16 *old, hunched teacher*

17 *beautifully clear, ice-cold pool*

18 *unsettled newborn baby*

19 *wet and tired children*

20 *brilliant, exciting, terrifying book*

21–28 Refer to definition of suffix in key words on page 1. Refer to Paper 2 Q22–29.

21 **grumpily**

22 **poorly**

23 **sadly**

24 **quickly**

25 **kindly**

26 **happily**

27 **stupidly**

28 **roughly**

29–30 **York, Newcastle** (line 3)

31 **north to south** (line 6)

32 **at Crewe** (lines 4–5)

33–34 Any two of: *Liverpool, Manchester, Sheffield, Salisbury, Exeter* (lines 5 & 8)

35 **excellent** (line 8)

36–40 Commas are used to separate the main clause in a sentence from the added information.

36–37 Harry, a very nervous boy, hated the thunderstorm. The main clause is 'Harry hated the thunderstorm' and 'a very nervous boy' is a noun phrase adding more information about Harry.

38 The boys set off along the track, anxious to get to the next village before dark. The main clause is 'The boys set off along the track' and 'anxious to get to the next village before dark' is an adverbial describing how the boys 'set off'.

39 Najib ran as fast as he could, barely taking a breath. The main clause is 'Najib ran as fast as he could' and 'barely taking a breath' is an adverbial describing how Najib ran.

40 Leena was starving, having not had anything to eat all day. The main clause is 'Leena was starving' and 'having not had anything to eat all day' is an adverbial describing why Leena was starving.

Paper 8 (pages 25–27)

1 **a place**

2 **ginger**

3 **fireflies** (line 18)

4 **green balls of pepper, red skies** (lines 6 & 17)

5 **rainy and sunny** (lines 12–14)

6 *They are worried about the rain, which washes away their houses. / They are waiting for the rain to stop so they can rebuild their houses.* (lines 13–16)

7 *The repeated 'z' in Zanzibar is like the sound buzzing bees.* (line 3)

8 *Yes, because the poet says: 'I didn't know it would smell of spice'; and includes details about the rain, the children and what the evenings were like.*

9–14 Refer to definition of noun in key words on page 1. An apostrophe and an 's' are placed after the name of whoever the noun belongs to.

9 It was **Dimitri's** rabbit.

10 They were **Jane's** crayons.

11 It was **Helen's** jacket.

12 It was **Mop's** bone.

13 It was **Rajeeh's** rat.

14 They were **Soraya's** books.

15–19 These words contain the short *i* sound spelt 'y'.

15 **myth**

16 **gym**

17 **Egypt**

18 **mystery**

19 **pyramid**

20–23 Refer to definitions of noun and plural in key words on page 1. Some of these nouns can't be made plural by adding '-s' or '-es' and are therefore irregular.
reindeer, grapefruit, goldfish, sheep

24–31 Refer to definition of synonym in key words on page 1.

24 **help**

25 **fall**

26 **unhappy**

27 **fast**

28 **some**

29 **like**

30 **new**

31 **leave**

32–37 Refer to definitions of plural and noun in key words on page 1. If a singular noun ends in 'f', it can be made plural by adding '-ves' (though there are some exceptions, e.g. roof, roofs).

32 hooves
33 shelves
34 loaves
35 calves
36 leaves
37 wolves

38–40 Possible answers include:
38 *My home has a swimming pool.*
39 *I have very frizzy hair.*
40 *My teacher is extremely tall.*

Paper 9 (pages 28–30)

1 False (it's brown ale)
2 False (it's to grease the basin)
3 False
4 True (ingredients: 1 large egg, beaten)
5 True (instruction 3)
6 False (it's to keep the saucer on tight)
7 False (instruction 2 says to leave for a day, instruction 5 says to steam for 6 hours, instruction 6 says to steam for another 2.5 hours)
8 *The pan will run out of water / will boil dry.* (instruction 5)

9–13 Refer to definition of verb in key words on page 1. Possible answers include:
9 *strolled*
10 *pleaded*
11 *grabbed*
12 *nagged*
13 *sprinted*

14–19

ch sounding 'sh' as in shout	ch sounding 'c' as in cat
chef	echo
machine	character
brochure	scheme

20–25 The sentences in the correct order read: A cyclist was knocked off his bicycle. The cyclist lay in the road. Meanwhile a policeman arrived. Then the policeman called for an ambulance. Next the ambulance arrived. Finally the cyclist was taken to hospital.
20 (2)
21 (4)
22 (1)
23 (6) Indicated by the adverb 'finally'.
24 (3)
25 (5)

26–31 Refer to definition of diminutive in key words on page 1.
26 owl – owlet
27 cat – kitten
28 goose – gosling
29 pig – piglet
30 duck – duckling
31 bull – bullock

32–40 Refer to Paper 1 Q32–40.
32–35 The plane landed at Heathrow Airport a little late.
36–40 Tessa and Claire admitted they were lost. What were they going to do?

Paper 10 (pages 30–32)

1 evening (title and line 8)
2 in a village (line 2)
3 beside the woods (line 7)
4–5 Two from: *the harness bells, the wind, the snow.* (lines 9 & 12)
6 *They are not near any houses, it is cold and dark.* (lines 6–8)
7 'The woods are lovely, dark and deep.' (line 13)
8 *I would feel scared of the woods because they were dark and you couldn't see what was hidden in them.*

9–16 Refer to definition of contraction in key words on page 1.
9 should have
10 will not
11 I will / I shall
12 cannot
13 they have
14 is not
15 would not
16 have not

17–22 Speech marks should be placed at the beginning of the speech and then at the end after the punctuation.
17 "Have you found the dog?" asked Jim.
18 "Let's go and play in the park," suggested Aman.
19 "I don't think you have washed your face!" joked Dad.
20 "Are you enjoying the pizza?" asked the waitress.
21 "I wish it would stop raining," sighed Amy.
22 "Where do you think you are going?" asked Mrs Thrower.

23–28 Refer to definition of suffix in key words on page 1. There is no hard and fast rule dictating which suffix to use.
23 suitable
24 reasonable

25 **sensible**
26 **believable**
27 **washable**
28 **responsible**
29–34 Refer to definition of adverb in key words on page 1. Adverbs commonly, but not always, end in '-ly'.
29 **angrily**
30 **noisily**
31 **slowly**
32 **neatly**
33 **sweetly**
34 **loudly**
35–40 Refer to definition of compound word in key words on page 1.
overhead, moonlight, somewhere, waterfall, drainpipe, classroom

Paper 11 (pages 33–35)

1 **by 438 BC** (lines 5–6)
2 **acid rain** (lines 12–13)
3 **hot in summer** (line 21)
4–5 Two of the following: *It is very large / a lot of people live there. It is lively and busy. There is a lot of traffic. There is a lot of air pollution.* (lines 8–11)
6 *It eats away at the marble of the ancient buildings.* (lines 12–13)
7 *It brought a new metro system and a new airport.* (line 17)
8 Possible answers: *I would not like to visit Athens as it is too crowded and polluted. I would like to visit Athens as it would be lively and fun.*
9–16 Refer to definition of proper noun in key words on page 1.
Thursday, River Thames, Kate, Queen Elizabeth, Jake, Mr Norton, September, London
17–22 Refer to definition of homonym in key words on page 1. Possible examples include:
17–18 *Dad tried to swat the fly. Rachel went to fly her kite.*
19–20 *My football match was cancelled. Uncle Tom lit the match.*
21–22 *The ball hit Sarah in the chest. I opened the chest in excitement.*
23–28 *Its* is a possessive determiner showing when something belongs to 'it'. *It's* is a contraction of 'it is'.
23 The cat jumped out of **its** bed.
24 "**It's** time we went to school," said Mum.
25 The elephant drank through **its** trunk.
26 "**It's** Sophie at the door, Amy," Dad shouted.

27–28 "**It's** autumn and time the tree lost **its** leaves," commented Nathan.
29–36 Any eight of: *child, blind, mild, kind, behind, hind, find, wind, wild*
37–40 Refer to definition of consonant letters in key words on page 1.
37 **elephant**
38 **lion**
39 **emu**
40 **giraffe**

Paper 12 (pages 36–38)

1 **Monday** (line 5)
2 **to pay properly** (lines 18–19)
3 **twelve** (line 26)
4 *She was frightened and she hated the C.I.S.* (lines 9–10)
5 *She nearly threw the mobile out of the window.* (lines 11–12)
6 Any one of: *Her dad had been out of work for a year. He was not in a good mood. He was tired. He was irritable and impatient.* (lines 27 & 32–34)
7 *They wouldn't understand. They would enjoy seeing her grovel.* (line 29)
8 *Because she wanted to ask her mother for money and so wanted to please her first.* (line 37)
9 Child's answer reflecting on how they would deal with the situation.
10–16 Refer to definition of homophone in key words on page 1.
10 I have never **seen** so many people there. One way to remember which homophone to use in this case is to note the word 'see' included in 'seen'.
11 The **bough** of the tree had broken off.
12 The man gave the queen a graceful **bow**.
13 There was a big **hole** in the ground.
14 The **whole** school went to see the play.
15–16 One way to remember which homophone to use in this case is to note the word 'eat' included in 'meat'.
15 The dog ate the **meat** in his bowl.
16 Jess said she'd **meet** Callum at the park.
17–22 Refer to Paper 8 Q9–14.
17 **the girl's jeans**
18 **my father's shoe**
19 **the child's toy**
20 **the dog's paw**
21 **Ravi's pencil**
22 **my gran's bracelet**
23–28 To work out whether to use 'sure' or 'ture', listen to the sound of the word. Words ending in 'sure' have a *sh* sound in the middle. Words ending in 'ture' do not.

23 **treasure**
24 **picture**
25 **adventure**
26 **measure**
27 **enclosure**
28 **creature**
29–35 Refer to definition of adjective in key words on page 1.
29 **shaggy**
30–31 **bright, blue**
32 **glistening**
33 **cosy**
34–35 **long, golden**
36–39 Refer to definition of verb in key words on page 1.
36 *shout*
37 *stare*
38 *march*
39 *scream*
40 *feel*

Paper 13 (pages 39–41)

1 **mudlarking** (line 5)
2 **coal** (line 2)
3 **a shilling** (line 22)
4 *It's a good time to hunt for coal and other things in the river.* (lines 1–2)
5 **a ship**
6 *Because he turned blue with cold / his hands and feet hurt.* (lines 8 & 12)
7 *Finding a big piece of coal.* (line 15)
8 *Old women (in Cotton Street or around All Saint's)* (lines 16–17)
9 Any one of: *It was difficult because of the cold, the difficulty of finding coal, having to wade in the Thames barefoot.*
10–15 Refer to Paper 1 Q32–40. As Wendy headed to the door she called, "Have you seen my hat?" (Child may add an additional comma after 'door'.)
16–22 Refer to definitions of plural and noun in key words on page 1. Apostrophes used to mark plural possession come after the plural noun, which often ends in '-s'.
16 **the three dogs' collars**
17 **the five girls' socks**
18 **the nine hens' eggs**
19 **the two cats' bowls**
20 **the four dolls' beds**
21 **the five boys' footballs**
22 **the three spiders' webs**
23–30 Refer to definition of verb and adverb in key words on page 1.
23–24 *slowly, quickly*

25–26 *peacefully, silently*
27–28 *messily, quickly*
29–30 *carefully, hastily*
31–35 **antique – unique, league – tongue, through – thought, vein – reign, chorus – echo**
36–40 Refer to definition of synonym in key words on page 1.
36 **dropped**
37 **hurry**
38 **different**
39 **under**
40 **select**

Paper 14 (pages 42–44)

1 **feed Izzy properly** (Denzil's letter, point 2)
2 **represent the class at the school council** (Ben's letter, paragraph 2)
3 **Dwayne** (Ben's letter, 3rd paragraph)
4 **a pet fish** (Denzil's letter, point 2)
5 Ben: either of: *He calmed down Mr Wilkinson; he hid Mrs Tollbart's specs.* (Ben's letter, paragraph 2)
Denzil: any one of: *He helped the class win the Tidy Books competition; he saved Izzy; he lent everyone his DVD; he asked Mr Wilkinson for afterschool football and netball.* (Denzil's letter, points 1, 2, 3 & 5)
6 Reasons might include: *Ben was rude about him in his letter; Ben nearly killed Izzy; Ben has not returned his DVD.*
7 Either letter could be chosen, but to gain a mark the child must provide a compelling reason for their choice.
8–15 Refer to definitions of nouns and plural in key words on page 1.
8 **bananas** Most singular words can be made plural by adding an 's'.
9 **foxes** If the plural ending sounds like *iz* and forms an extra syllable or 'beat' in the word, it is spelt as '-es'.
10 **lorries** Words ending in a consonant + 'y' can be made plural by changing the 'y' to 'ies'.
11 **trays** Refer to Q8.
12 **churches** Refer to Q9.
13 **brushes** Refer to Q9.
14 **girls** Refer to Q8.
15 **beaches** Refer to Q9.
16–21 Refer to Paper 7 Q36–40.
16 First thing this morning, we met for a swim with our new friends. The main clause is 'we met for a swim with our new friends' and 'First thing this morning' is an adverbial describing when they went for a swim.

17 Later that day, Daniel's gran did a magic trick. The main clause is 'Daniel's gran did a magic trick' and 'Later that day' is an adverbial describing when she did the magic trick.

18 Although her face didn't show it, she was very unhappy. The main clause is 'she was very unhappy' and 'Although her face didn't show it' is a subordinate clause.

19 Her eyes drowsy with sleep, Fran dozed off. The main clause is 'Fran dozed off' and 'Her eyes drowsy with sleep' is an adverbial describing how Fran dozed off.

20 Looking for his home, the dog ran on ahead. The main clause is 'the dog ran on ahead' and 'Looking for his home' is an adverbial describing how the dog ran on ahead.

21 Groping in the dark, Sam found the light switch. The main clause is 'Sam found the light switch' and 'Groping in the dark' is an adverbial describing how Sam found the light switch.

22 **princess**

23 **duchess**

24 **wife**

25 **aunt**

26 **she**

27 **niece**

28 **sister**

29–34 Refer to definition of adjectival phrase in key words on page 1.

29 The <u>**large, brown**</u> clock hung on the wall.

30 The <u>**bright, loud, flashing**</u> fireworks exploded in the air.

31 Sam, the <u>**long-haired, shaggy**</u> dog, loved going for a walk.

32 The <u>**stern, pale-faced**</u> teacher glared at the children.

33 Caroline's coat, <u>**soaked and muddy**</u>, didn't look new any more.

34 Rain poured from the <u>**grey, heavy**</u> clouds.

35–40 Refer to definition of pronoun in key words on page 1. Possible answers include:

35 *I went to the park.*

36 *That bag is ours.*

37 *Give it to him.*

38 *The cup is mine.*

39 *Can they come too?*

40 *She is very fast.*

6–7 *It was travelling very fast. It stopped in front of the sun and formed a perfect circle around Philip.* (lines 22–23 & 29)

8 *The kite moved in his hand and wagged its tail like a dog's when it sees a friend.* (lines 23–25)

9–16 Refer to definition of noun in key words on page 1.
gatepost, bunch, Wednesday, Tom, Edinburgh, Edward, freedom, stream

17–22 Refer to Paper 4 Q16–20.

17 "Come quickly!" screamed Sam.

18 "How are you, Gran?" asked Peter.

19 "It's time to go," sighed Mum.

20 "This way to the Tunnel of Screams," directed the attendant.

21 "Have we got time?" enquired Nancy.

22 "Where are my slippers?" exclaimed Grandad.

23–27 Refer to definition of adverb in key words on page 1.

23 The soldier stood **here**, guarding the palace.

24 The nurse removed the dressing **gently**.

25 The ducks in the pond quacked **loudly**.

26 The old man **cheerfully** greeted his friend.

27 The boys pushed past her **then** ran off laughing.

28–33 Refer to definition of suffix in key words on page 1. Clues about whether to put 't', 's', 'ss' or 'c' before the suffix '-ion' often come from the last letter or letters of the root word.

28 **expression** '-ssion' is used if the root word ends in 'ss' (i.e. express)

29 **information** The suffix '-ation' is added to verbs to form nouns (i.e. inform)

30 **discussion** Refer to Q28 (i.e. discuss).

31 **extension** '-sion' is used if the root words ends in 'd' (i.e. extend).

32 **education** '-tion' is used if the root word ends in 'te' (i.e. educate). Also refer to Q29.

33 **pollution** Refer to Q29 and Q32 (i.e. pollute).

34–40 Refer to definition of antonym in key words on page 1. Possible answers include:

34 *sad*

35 *small*

36 *drop*

37 *quiet*

38 *thick / fat*

39 *below*

40 *up*

Paper 15 (pages 45–48)

1 **China** (line 8)

2 **his bedroom** (line 13)

3 **three** (line 18)

4 *that his dad was being a spoil-sport* (line 15)

5 *His arms ached and he was out of breath.* (lines 19 & 21)

Paper 16 (pages 49–51)

1 **Shelborn Avenue** (bullet point 1, lines 1–2)

2 **the sea** (bullet point 2, lines 1–2)

3 **a tower** (bullet point 4, line 2)

4 **long** (bullet point 3, line 2)

5 (1) **Shelborn** (bullet point 1, lines 1–2)
(2) **River** (bullet point 1, line 2)

(3) **Harbour** (bullet point 2, line 1)

(4) **Oaktree** (bullet point 2, line 3)

(5) **Mill** (bullet point 3, line 2)

6 **River Road** (bullet point 1, lines 2–3)

7 **Ride a bike** (bullet point 2, line 6)

8 **58 Mill Road, Denton** (line 2 of letter; bullet point 3 line 2; bullet point 4 line 3)

9 **Pirates** (in the PS)

10–15 Refer to definition of conjunction in key words on page 1.

10 He tried to open the door **although** he had seen the man lock it.

11 I would rather have a cup of hot tea **than** drink a mug of cold coffee.

12 I cut my hand **so** I put a plaster on it.

13 Joe wanted to buy some sweets **but / although** he hadn't brought enough money.

14 I shall wear a T-shirt **if** it is a warm day.

15 The girls are going hiking **and** swimming.

16–23 Refer to definition of syllable in key words on page 1.

16 **bub / ble**

17 **pad / dle**

18 **flan / nel**

19 **ken / nel**

20 **ar / rive**

21 **sad / dle**

22 **bur / row**

23 **cab / bage**

24–31 Refer to definition of adjective in key words on page 1. The spelling of <u>these</u> root words <u>do</u> not need to be changed when adding these suffixes' so there is no confusion and the child doesn't think they never have to change the root word when adding these suffixes.

	add 'er'	add 'est'
short	shorter	shortest
high	higher	highest
small	smaller	smallest
slow	slower	slowest

32–35 These words all contain an *s* sound spelt 'sc'.

32 s<u>c</u>ene

33 dis<u>c</u>ipline

34 fas<u>c</u>inate

35 cres<u>c</u>ent

36 **snow – cow**

37 **pull – skull**

38 **ear – wear**

39 **wave – have**

40 **bough – trough**

Paper 17 (pages 52–54)

1 **no** (line 1)

2 **some of them** (lines 3–4)

3 **Billy** (lines 7–8)

4–5 *They call him names. They make up jokes about his mum.* (lines 5–6)

6 *They don't really mean it.* (line 11)

7–9 *lonely, upset, angry*

10–16 Refer to definition of compound word in key words on page 1.

10 **hand + bag**

11 **sun + light**

12 **candle + stick**

13 **shoe + lace**

14 **tooth + paste**

15 **dust + bin**

16 **post + box**

17–22 Refer to definition of prefix in key words on page 1.

re	de	pre
replay	deflate	prehistoric
revisit	demist	precaution

23–28 Refer to definition of phrase in key words on page 1. Refer to Paper 8 Q9–14 and Paper 13 Q16–20. Possible answers include:

23–24 *You must not disturb this bird's chicks.*

25–26 *The boy stole that girl's sweets.*

27–28 *Can we use those boys' pencils?*

29–33 Antony likes playing football (because 'Antony likes outdoor games')
Brian likes painting (because 'Brian is artistic')
Brian likes craft lessons (because 'he likes making things')
The other boys like Antony (because 'he is very popular with the other boys')
Antony would rather play cricket than stay indoors. (because 'Antony likes outdoor games')

34–40 Refer to definitions of noun, adjective, verb and adverb in key words on page 1.
nouns: **Thursday, scream**
adjectives: **windy, loud**
verbs: **walking, heard**
adverbs: **briskly**

Paper 18 (pages 55–58)

1 **the fashion for longer hair and beards** (lines 2–3)

2 **she did not have enough to eat** (line 4)

3 **a palm tree** (line 19)

4–5 Two from: *he needed to get some money; he was stung by his wife's words; he did not like being hit with a broom.* (lines 9–11)

6 *The barber was disturbing him by being on its territory.* (line 18)

7 *His legs shook, his hair stood straight up, his teeth chattered.* (lines 24–25 & 27)

8 *He remained calm / he was able to think clearly.*

9 *The barber would use the mirror to show the ghost its reflection to make it think the barber had captured another ghost.*

10–14 Refer to definitions of noun, plural and singular in key words on page 1.

10 **aircraft**

11–12 **scissors, clothes**

13 **bison**

14 **sheep**

15–20 Sometimes the root word is obvious and the usual rules apply for adding suffixes beginning with vowel letters (no change to root word), as in 'poisonous'. Sometimes there is no obvious root word, as in 'tremendous' and 'jealous'. In words like 'humorous', '-our' is changed to '-or' before '-ous' is added. A final 'e' of the root word must be kept if the *j* sound of 'g' is to be kept, as in 'courageous'. If there is a long *e* sound before the '-ous' ending, it is usually spelt as 'i', as in 'curious', but a few words have 'e', as in 'hideous'.
poisonous, curious, jealous, hideous, humorous, tremendous

21–28 An exclamation mark is used to show when something is urgent or surprising. It can also be used at the end of an order or instruction. A question mark comes after a question.

21 Catch the thief!

22 Shall we look in this shop?

23 Don't do that!

24 Why does Dad snore so loudly?

25 Can we go swimming now?

26 Hurry up, time is running out!

27 Listen, a siren!

28 Please may I have a sweet?

29–34 **camcorder, DVD player, astronaut, television, microwave**
The word 'cinema' was in common use as early as 1914. Other words – e.g. television (first used in 1900), astronaut (first used in 1929) and microwave (first used in 1931) – were written down long before the inventions to which they refer became reality, but most people would not have heard of them or used them back then.

35–40 Refer to definition of pronoun in key words on page 1.

Pronouns about others	Pronouns about myself
yours	me
hers	I
theirs	mine

1 **going to catch a bus** (line 3)

2 **nervous** (line 10)

3 **twilight** (line 1: 5.20pm; line 5: streetlights starting to come on)

4 *He couldn't keep his hands still.* (line 13)

5 *The assistants were taking things out of the window.* (lines 20–22)

6–7 *The witness was not quite sure of the exact time and could not remember the colour of the man's hair.* (lines 1–2 & 12)

8 *The witness says that the tall man was wearing the baseball cap, but earlier the witness said the shorter man was wearing the baseball cap.* (lines 15 & 31)

9–17 Refer to Paper 2 Q16–21.

9–10 Aman has to buy carrots, potatoes, rice and tomatoes at the shop.

11–13 At the park Geri, Meena, David, Jason and John all play together. (The child may also place a comma after the word 'park'.)

14–15 On Mark's way to school he passes the police station, the swimming pool, the park and the shops. (The child may also place a comma after the word 'school'.)

16–17 At the farm the children fed the goats, stroked the pigs, milked the cows and brushed the horse. (The child may also place a comma after the word 'farm'.)

18–25 Refer to definitions of adjective and suffix in key words on page 1. When adding a suffix to one-syllable words with a short vowel sound, the last consonant should be doubled.

	add 'er'	add 'est'
hot	hotter	hottest
tall	taller	tallest
big	bigger	biggest
thin	thinner	thinnest

26–29 Refer to definition of diminutive in key words on page 1.

26 **droplet**

27 **duckling**

28 **bullock**

29 **booklet**

30–35 Refer to Paper 1 Q32–40. Max asked, "Is it time Jess got out of bed?"

36–40 'Their' is a possessive determiner showing who the noun belongs to. 'There' is a pronoun indicating place (note the word 'here' inside 'there' as a way of remembering the difference between these homophones).

36 The children went to play with **their** friends in the swimming pool.

37 **There** isn't going to be any rain today.

38–39 **Their** shoes are over **there** on the floor.

40 **There** was a huge bang as the fireworks exploded.

Paper 20 (pages 62–65)

1 **ask no questions** (line 3)
2 **smugglers** (title)
3 **brushwood** (line 14)
4 **midnight** (line 1)
5 **brandy, 'baccy (tobacco), laces, letters, barrels of brandy-wine** (lines 7–9 & 12)
6 *So that you don't see the smugglers.*
7 **tar and ropes** (line 12)
8 *The poem refers to 'your mother' and uses the phrases 'my darling' and 'for your play'.*

9–12 Refer to definition of suffix in key words on page 1.
9 **friendship**
10 **neighbourhood**
11 **motherhood**
12 **apprenticeship**

13–20 Refer to Paper 11 Q23–28.
13 **It's** a beautiful day.
14 The cat played with **its** ball.

15–16 **It's** time you remembered your own bag, **it's** not that hard.
17 Everyone was lined up outside the school; **its** fire alarm was going.
18 Will's dog lost **its** ball.
19 **It's** got to be here somewhere.
20 **It's** been a brilliant party. I wish I could have one every week!

21–27 Refer to definition of phrase in key words on page 1. The phrase could start with a determiner (e.g. the, a, an) but should include adjectives (listed with commas if there's more than one). Possible answers include:
21 *the long, warm coat*
22 *the huge, grey elephant*
23 *the fast, red car*
24 *the giant, pointed skyscraper*
25 *the gnarled, old tree*
26 *the hard-boiled egg*
27 *the limp, wilting flower*

28–34 Refer to definition of conjunction in key words on page 1.
28 I missed the train **because / after** I overslept.
29 Ahmed is in the cricket team **but / because** Josh wasn't good enough.
30 Mum wrapped up my present **after / and** I went to bed.
31 Jake bought some toffees **and / so** Mike got some too.
32 Cathy's sewing is untidy **so / and** she will have to do it again.
33 I like macaroni **but** my brother likes spaghetti better.
34 The sky was blue **and / because** the sun was shining.

35–40 Refer to definition of definition in key words on page 1.
35 **herd**
36 **adult**
37 **sleepy**
38 **cautious**
39 **error**
40 **soon**

A Visitor's Guide to Athens

Athens is one of the oldest of all cities. Named after Athena, the Greek goddess of wisdom, its history stretches back over 3000 years. It is home to one of the world's most famous buildings. The white marble temple, the Parthenon, sits on a hill right in the centre of the city. It can be seen for miles around. It took about eight years to build and was completed in   *5* 438 BC. It is one of the main reasons why tourists visit Athens.

However, when visitors come to modern Athens for the first time they are rather surprised by what they find. Athens is very big. About 4 million people live there. It is a lively, modern, busy place with many urban problems. There are huge traffic jams in the city's streets and   *10* considerable air pollution. Sometimes the smog is so thick that it is almost impossible to see the Parthenon on its hill. Acid rain is eating away at the marble of the ancient buildings and has already caused irreversible damage.

Fortunately in the last few years there have been some improvements   *15* in the air quality. In preparation for the Olympic Games, which were staged in Athens in 2004, the city built a new metro system. The rail network carries 400,000 passengers a day. It is estimated to have removed 200,000 cars from the streets. For the Games Athens also built a wonderful new airport on the edge of the city.   *20*

Athens has very hot summers. In July and August the average daytime temperature is 31°C. Athenians tend to stay out late at night when it's cooler. No one eats much before 9 pm, and many shows and entertainments don't start until midnight. You need to be able to stay up late in Athens! Winters, on the other hand, can be quite cold and the city   *25* has snowfalls most years. The best times to come are spring and autumn – and there's lots to do: museums, art galleries, restaurants and nightlife. And if you get tired of it all, take the metro to the city's port and hop on a boat to one of the hundreds of Greek islands where you can lie in the sun and get away from the crowds.   *30*

Underline the right answers.

1 When was the Parthenon built?

(by 438 BC, 3000 years ago, we don't know)

2 The ancient buildings are damaged by (tourists, earthquakes, acid rain).

3 The climate in Athens is (wet, warm all the year round, hot in summer).

Answer these questions.

4–5 List two things that surprise visitors to Athens.

____

____

6 Why is acid rain so damaging?

____

7 What benefits did the 2004 Olympic Games bring to Athens?

____

8 Explain why you would or would not like to visit Athens, using information from the visitor's guide.

____

Underline all the **proper nouns**.

9–16 ten   Thursday   River Thames   cat   Kate   lunch

Queen Elizabeth   tonight   Jake   Mr Norton

September   line   London

Write two sentences for each **homonym**. In each sentence the homonym must have a different meaning.

17–18 fly

(1) ____

(2) ____

19–20 match

    (1) ____

    (2) ____

21–22 chest

    (1) ____

    (2) ____

Add *its* or *it's* to fill the gap in each sentence. Don't forget to use a capital letter where necessary.

23 The cat jumped out of __________ bed.

24 "__________ time we went to school," called Mum.

25 The elephant drank through __________ trunk.

26 "__________ Sophie at the door, Amy," Dad shouted.

27–28 "__________ autumn and time the tree lost __________ leaves," commented Nathan.

Find eight words in the wordsearch ending in *ild* or *ind*.

b	c	h	i	l	d	t
l	g	k	n	d	s	a
i	g	o	w	t	j	f
n	r	f	i	i	h	i
d	m	i	l	d	n	n
k	i	n	d	s	e	d
s	b	e	h	i	n	d

29–36 __________ __________ __________ __________

        __________ __________ __________ __________

Add the missing **consonant letters** to each word to make a wild animal.

37 e__e__ __a__ __   **38** __io__

39 e__u   **40** __i__a__ __e .

Mia is being bullied at school by a gang called the C.I.S.

On Saturday morning they woke me up at a quarter past seven.

Their text message was short and not at all sweet.

PAY UP ON MON OR ELSE   5

After seeing that I couldn't stop shaking. In the end I put the blankets over my head and curled up tightly into a ball.

Oh how I hated their messages. Hated them, hated them, HATED THEM. In fact,   10
I nearly got up and threw my mobile out of the window. Then I stopped myself, because that would have been a daft thing to do – and anyway, they'd just love me to do that.   15

So instead I lay under my covers worrying about Monday … What were we going to do? We'd joked about handing them fake money or giving them the five pounds all in two-pence pieces. But I was pretty certain we'd hand over the money. It seemed the easiest and safest option – for now.

I had just one problem with that. I was flat broke.   20

I'd insisted on paying Oliver back the four pounds he'd loaned me. And the rest – which wasn't much – I'd spent on sweets and a magazine.

Of course, I could ask Oliver to lend me another five pounds. And I knew he would. But that just seemed to be taking advantage of his good nature. What else could I do? Well, I could always try and explain to the   25 C.I.S. that I only get twelve pounds a month pocket money. And remind them again that my dad was out of work for a year.

It would all just be a waste of my breath, though. Chris Freyer would enjoy seeing me grovel to her. But she wouldn't understand. That chip on her shoulder was so huge it blotted out everything else. So it seemed I   30 had no choice but to put out the begging bowl to my parents.

My dad was home now, but he was not in the best of moods. I think he was just dead tired with his new job and all the training he'd just done, but he was kind of irritable and impatient. Then, in the afternoon he took my two little brothers swimming: this was the moment to work on   35 my mum.

To butter her up I offered to do the hoovering downstairs. I did it extra thoroughly too.

From *Traitor* by Pete Johnson

Underline the right answers.

1 The gang told Mia to pay on (Monday, Tuesday, Wednesday, Thursday).

2 She decided (not to pay, to give them fake money, only to pay in two-pence pieces, to pay properly).

3 For pocket money she got (four, five, twelve) pounds a month.

Answer these questions.

4 Why couldn't Mia stop shaking?

____

5 What did Mia nearly do?

____

6 Why was it hard to ask her dad for money?

____

7 Explain in your own words why it was a waste of time explaining to the gang that she could not pay.

____

8 Why did Mia do the hoovering extra thoroughly?

____

9 What would you do if you were being asked for money?

____

Underline the correct **homophone** in the brackets.

10 I have never (seen, scene) so many people there.

11 The (bough, bow) of the tree had broken off.

12 The man gave the queen a graceful (bough, bow).

13 There was a big (hole, whole) in the ground.

14 The (hole, whole) school went to see the play.

15 The dog ate the (meet, meat) in his bowl.

16 Jess said she'd (meet, meat) Callum at the park.

Write the following lines in a shortened form, using the apostrophe.

Example: the glove belonging to the lady   *the lady's glove*

17 the jeans worn by the girl   _______________________

18 the shoe belonging to my father   _______________________

19 the toy the child had   _______________________

20 the paw of the dog   _______________________

21 the pencil Ravi owned   _______________________

22 the bracelet belonging to my gran   _______________________   6

Add sure or ture to these letters to make a word.

23 trea________   24 pic________

25 adven________   26 mea________

27 enclo________   28 crea________   6

Underline the **adjectives** in each sentence.

29 The shaggy dog panted loudly.

30–31 Tom's bright blue coat suited him well.

32 The glistening raindrops hung on the branches.

33 Naomi slept in her cosy bed.

34–35 Donna's long, golden hair had all been cut off!   7

Write a more powerful **verb** for each of these verbs.

Example: take   *grab*

36 say   _______________   37 look   _______________

38 walk   _______________   39 call   _______________

40 touch   _______________   5

Paper 13

This story is set in Victorian London. Jamie and his friends make a living hunting for scraps beside the Thames.

Low tide was early next morning.

I'm a mudlark. I make my money by picking up the coal that falls out when they're unloading the brigs. I have a little basket strapped to my back. Sometimes I fill it twice in a day. Not that often, though.

I'm a good worker. I go out mudlarking even in the winter when most of the others can't stand the cold. It was only me and Davies and Ten Tons and maybe Patty and a couple of others by Blackwall pier this winter. Ten Tons and me are fine with it, but Davies turns blue with cold. I'm tougher than Davies, even though he's stronger than me. I can work all day even in the winter, when you have to crack the ice to lever the coals out of the mud. It's all Davies can do to sit on the bank and shiver and cry because his hands and feet hurt so much.

Sometimes the coal lies on the surface of the mud, but often it sinks under. Then you have to feel in the thick mud with your toes and hands. It's exciting when you find a big piece, but it's usually little nibs. When the basket's full I take it and sell my coal to the old women up and down Cotton Street or around All Saint's.

We don't just pick up coals, we pick up anything that gets dropped, just about. You get a farthing a pound for old iron. You get ha'pence for bits of rope. If you find fat the cooks have dropped overboard you can get three farthings for that. For good new copper, you can get up to four pence a pound.

Most things can be sold in this world. Once I made a shilling in a day. Mostly it's more like seven or eight pence.

From *The Copper Treasure* by Melvin Burgess

Underline the right answers.

1 What word is used to describe what the children in the story do?

(treasure hunting, mudlarking, scavenging)

2 What are they looking to find in the river?

(coal, gold, rubber)

5
10
15
20

3 What was the most Jamie ever made in a day? (four pence, a shilling, seven pence, eight pence).

3

Answer these questions.

4 Write in your own words why low tide was important to Jamie.

____

5 What is a 'brig' (line 3)?

____

6 Why did Davies find it so hard to work in winter?

____

7 What excited Jamie when he was out mudlarking?

____

8 Who bought the coal from Jamie?

____

9 Explain in your own words why mudlarking was so hard.

____

6

Write this sentence again, adding the missing punctuation and capital letters.

10–15 as Wendy headed to the door she called have you seen my hat

____

____

6

Add the missing apostrophes to these **plural nouns**.

Example: the six boys books   the six boys' books

16 the three dogs collars   _______________________

17 the five girls socks   _______________________

18 the nine hens eggs   _______________________

19 the two cats bowls   _______________________

20 the four dolls beds   _______________________

21 the five boys footballs _______________________________

22 the three spiders webs _______________________________   7

Next to each **verb** write two **adverbs** that could describe it.

23–24 walk   _______________   _______________

25–26 sleep   _______________   _______________

27–28 eat   _______________   _______________

29–30 draw   _______________   _______________   8

31–35 Match the words with the same spelling patterns using a line.

    antique   echo

    league   reign

    through   unique

    chorus   thought

    vein   tongue   5

Underline a **synonym** for the word in bold.

36 fell	dropped	flew	rose	felt
37 rush	blow	bump	knock	hurry
38 unlike	different	same	unkind	similar
39 beneath	above	beyond	away	under
40 choose	like	eat	select	present

    5

Vote for Ben Barton!

Just writing to let you know it's time to choose the Form Captain again. Yes, I know it's a dreadful bore thinking about it, but to save your tiny brains the effort, I've got a dead simple solution – vote for me, Ben Barton, the number one choice for Form Five.

Why? Easy! Who came top of exams last year? Who's the leading goal scorer in the school team? Who knows how to calm Mr Wilkinson down when he's in a mood? Who hid Mrs Tollbart's specs so she couldn't mark our homework last week? Who will represent you best at the school council, as long as you pay me (just joking!)? Who can do juggling tricks with the bean bags?

And just think what the alternatives are! Sally Hunt – the biggest airhead in the class? Dwayne 'the Gorilla' Smith? I don't think so. Denzil Steel-Perkins? With a name like that he'd better stay class librarian. There's really only one choice – me! So vote, vote, vote for Brainy Ben, I say!

Dear Fellow Class Members

I'm writing to ask for your vote in the elections for Form Captain. I realise it's hard to decide who to vote for. It's easy to choose your best friend, or the person who shouts loudest, but it's best to choose someone who will help the whole class. I'd like to give you five reasons for considering me.

1   I kept the class library in perfect shape last year so that we won the Tidy Books competition.
2   I saved Izzy from eating himself to death when someone (whose initials begin with BB) put too much food in his water tank.
3   I lent everyone in the class my Supertronics DVD last term, though I'm still waiting for it back from The Person Who Overfed Izzy.
4   I will campaign for an extra five minutes at break time.
5   I have already asked Mr Wilkinson if we can have afterschool footie and netball.

Whoever you vote for, I'll still be your friend.

Best wishes

Denzil

Underline the right answers.

1 Which of these things can Ben not do?

(play football, juggle, feed Izzy properly, calm down Mr Wilkinson)

2 The form captain has to:

(tidy the library, feed Izzy, represent the class at the school council, juggle beanbags).

3 Who was called 'the Gorilla'?

(Sally, Denzil, Dwayne, Izzy, Ben)

Answer these questions.

4 Who or what is Izzy?

____

5 List something each boy has already done to help the class.

Ben _______________________________________

Denzil _____________________________________

6 Explain in your own words why Denzil might not like Ben.

____

7 Whose letter is more persuasive? Give reasons for your choice.

____

Write each of these **nouns** in their **plural** form.

8 banana _________________   **9** fox _________________

10 lorry _________________   **11** tray _________________

12 church _________________   **13** brush _________________

14 girl _________________   **15** beach _________________

Add the missing comma to each of these sentences.

16 First thing this morning we met for a swim with our new friends.

17 Later that day Daniel's gran did a magic trick.

18 Although her face didn't show it she was very unhappy.

19 Her eyes drowsy with sleep Fran dozed off.

20 Looking for his home the dog ran on ahead.

21 Groping in the dark Sam found the light switch.

Underline the feminine word for the word in bold.

22 prince   fairy   woman   princess   queen

23 duke   player   actress   lady   duchess

24 husband   mother   father   wife   aunt

25 uncle   nephew   aunt   niece   sister

26 he   her   him   them   she

27 nephew   uncle   niece   cousin   woman

28 brother   sister   mother   child   twin

Underline the **adjectival phrase** in each sentence.

29 The large, brown clock hung on the wall.

30 The bright, loud, flashing fireworks exploded in the air.

31 Sam, the long-haired, shaggy dog, loved going for a walk.

32 The stern, pale-faced teacher glared at the children.

33 Caroline's coat, soaked and muddy, didn't look new any more.

34 Rain poured from the grey, heavy clouds.

Use each of these **pronouns** in a sentence.

35 I

____

36 ours

____

37 him

____

38 mine

____

39 they

____

40 she

____

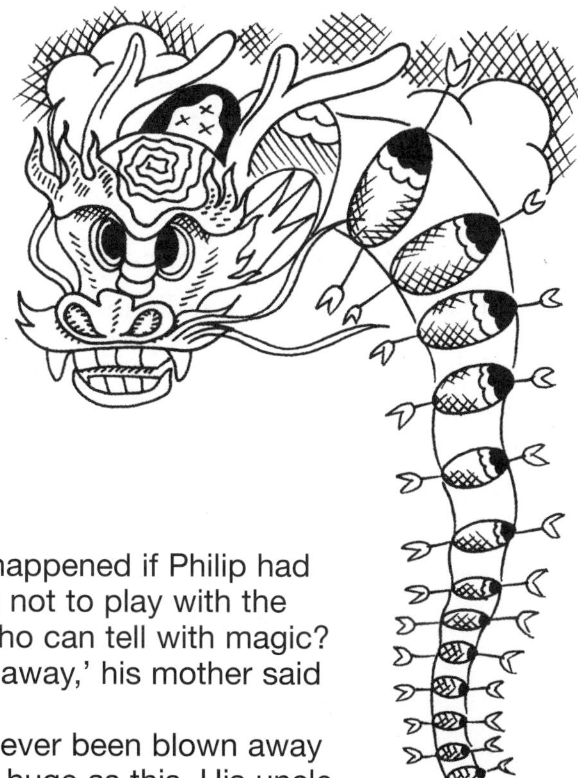

Maybe none of it would have happened if Philip had listened to his father's warning not to play with the kite on his own. Maybe. But who can tell with magic?

'It's big enough to blow you away,' his mother said when she saw the kite.

Philip laughed. Nobody had ever been blown away on a kite – not even on one as huge as this. His uncle had brought it back as a present from China and it really was the biggest and best you'd ever seen. It was shaped like a dragon and was coloured red, yellow and green.

Philip wanted to go out and fly it at once but his father said he had to wait until the weekend. The weekend! That was a whole four days away.

Philip put the kite in the corner of his bedroom. Every time he looked at it, he heard a voice whispering in his head.

'Go on,' the voice said, 'it's your kite. Dad's just a spoil-sport. Go on – it'll be good fun. No one will know if you sneak out for half an hour.'

For two days Philip managed to say 'no' to the voice, but on the third day he gave in …

The kite was so big that his arms ached from holding it up so that it didn't touch the ground. It was so big that by the time he reached the top of the hill in the park he was out of breath …

He looked up. A small, round, black cloud was racing across the blue sky. It was moving faster than any cloud Philip had ever seen. He felt the kite move in his hand. The long dragon's tail wagged from side to side like a dog's when it sees a friend.

The cloud got nearer and nearer the sun. Philip saw its shadow come racing up the hill towards him. It grew darker and Philip waited for the shadow to pass. But when he looked up, the cloud had stopped, directly in front of the sun. Its shadow formed a perfect circle all around him.

Then, out of nowhere came the wind. Whistling and spinning and howling. Philip closed his eyes. He felt his arms rise up above him as the wind caught the kite and lifted it. For a moment, he thought of letting go but there was a sudden tug and it was too late.

From *Beaver Towers* by Nigel Hinton

Underline the right answers.

1 The kite came from (Peru, China, France, America).

2 Philip kept the kite in (the garage, the kitchen, his bedroom).

3 Philip gave in to the voice after (four, three, two, five) days.

Answer these questions.

4 What did the voice try to make Philip think about his father?

____

5 How did Philip feel as he carried the kite to the park?

____

6–7 What two things were very unusual about the cloud's behaviour?

(1) ____

(2) ____

8 What, in the story, tells you that there was a connection between the kite and the cloud?

____

Circle words that are **nouns**.

9–16   gatepost   happy   bunch   laughed

        Wednesday   greasy   sadly   Tom

        Edinburgh   Edward   freedom

        stream   famous   fought

Rewrite these sentences, adding the missing speech marks.

17 Come quickly! screamed Sam.

____

18 How are you, Gran? asked Peter.

____

19 It's time to go, sighed Mum.

____

20 This way to the Tunnel of Screams, directed the attendant.

____

21 Have we got time? enquired Nancy.

____

22 Where are my slippers? exclaimed Grandad.

____   6

Choose the most suitable **adverb** from the words below to put in each space. Each word may only be used once.

cheerfully   then   gently   here   loudly

23 The soldier stood _______________, guarding the palace.

24 The nurse removed the dressing _______________.

25 The ducks in the pond quacked _______________.

26 The old man _______________ greeted his friend.

27 The boys pushed past her _______________ ran off laughing.   5

Add the **suffix** _ion_ to each word, but be careful as some letters may need to be removed or added.

Example: explode + ion = explosion

28 express + ion = ______________

29 inform + ion = ______________

30 discuss + ion = ______________

31 extend + ion = ______________

32 educate + ion = ______________

33 pollute + ion = ______________ 6

Write an **antonym** of each word.

34 happy ______________   **35** large ______________

36 catch ______________   **37** noisy ______________

38 thin ______________   **39** above ______________

40 down ______________ 7

Dear Gail

As you live near me in Denton, here are directions for getting to my party on foot:

*   Go out of your gate. Turn left. Go to the end of Shelborn Avenue. Turn right into River Road. Go as far as the post-box. Cross the road there. (Be careful. Cars come fast up the road.) Go down the footpath opposite, past the horse field. (Usually two old ponies in there, very keen on carrots!)

*   At the end you're in Harbour Road. Don't take the right to the sea front. Turn left, go past St James Church with the spire, cross the road again, take the third right into Oaktree Road. (There's a house with a red gate just before the turn.) Go about 90 metres until you see a sign on the right hand side that says 'Public Footpath, no bicycles'. Don't take this. Just beyond there's another path between two very tall houses. It's not marked at all.

*   Go down there, over the footbridge. When you get to the end, you're in our road, Mill Road. It's a very long road, so you've still got a way to go.

*   Turn left. Keep going until you see the second church, St John's, on the right, with a tower. Our house is seven beyond that, number 58. It's got a holly hedge and balloons outside.

*   It should take you about 20 minutes. Any problems just ring on your mobile. Our number is 552961.

See you there!

Imran

P.S. I'm sure everyone in Denton will think you wearing a pirate hat in public is quite normal!

Underline the right answers.

1 Gail lives in (Harbour Road, Mill Road, Shelborn Avenue, River Road).

2 Gail lives near (a motorway, the sea, a supermarket).

3 St John's church has (a tower, a spire, a flag).

4 Mill Road is (long, dangerous, straight).

Answer these questions.

5 Write down these roads in the order that Gail will travel along them:

Oaktree, River, Harbour, Mill, Shelborn.

(1) _______________   (2) _______________   (3) _______________

(4) _______________   (5) _______________

6 Where would you go to post a letter?

____

7 What can't you do on the footpath in Oaktree Road?

____

8 What address does Imran live at? Include the name of the town.

____

9 What was the fancy dress theme for the party?

____

Put one of the **conjunctions** in each of the spaces below.

but   although   than   and   if   so

10 He tried to open the door _________ he had seen the man lock it.

11 I would rather have a cup of hot tea _________ drink a mug of cold coffee.

12 I cut my hand _________ I put a plaster on it.

13 Joe wanted to buy some sweets _________ he hadn't brought enough money.

14 I shall wear a T-shirt _________ it is a warm day.

15 The girls are going hiking _________ swimming.

Rewrite these words, drawing a line to separate the **syllables**.

Example: yellow   yel/low

16 bubble _______________   17 paddle _______________

18 flannel _______________   19 kennel _______________

20 arrive _______________   21 saddle _______________

22 burrow _______________   23 cabbage _______________

Complete this table of comparing **adjectives**.

24–31

	add 'er'	add 'est'
short		
high		
small		
slow		

Circle the silent letter in each of these words.

32 scene   33 discipline

34 fascinate   35 crescent

With a line, match the words that have the same letter string (group of letters) but which make a different sound.

36 snow   have

37 pull   trough

38 ear   skull

39 wave   cow

40 bough   wear

Paper 17

Billy Doesn't Like School Really

Billy doesn't like school really.
It's not because he can't do the work
but because some of the other kids
don't seem to like him that much.

They call him names
and make up jokes about his mum.

Everyone laughs ... except Billy.
Everyone laughs ... except Billy.

They all think it's OK
because it's only a laugh and a joke
and they don't really mean it anyway
but Billy doesn't know that.

Billy doesn't know that
and because of that
Billy doesn't like school really.

by Paul Cookson

Underline the right answers.

1 Does Billy like school?
(yes, no, don't know)

2 How many children don't like Billy?
(all of them, some of them, none of them)

Answer these questions.

3 Who doesn't laugh in this poem?

4–5 What two things do the other children do to Billy?

(1) _______________________________________

(2) _______________________________________

2

6 Why do all the children think it is OK to have a laugh and a joke?

____

7–9 Write three words describing how you would feel if you were Billy.

___________   ___________   ___________

Write the two small words each **compound word** is made from.

10 handbag   =   ___________ + ___________

11 sunlight   =   ___________ + ___________

12 candlestick   =   ___________ + ___________

13 shoelace   =   ___________ + ___________

14 toothpaste   =   ___________ + ___________

15 dustbin   =   ___________ + ___________

16 postbox   =   ___________ + ___________

Write these words, depending on their **prefix**, in the table below.

deflate   replay   demist   prehistoric   revisit   precaution

17–22

re	de	pre

Write each of these **phrases** in a sentence and don't forget the missing apostrophe.

23–24 this birds chicks

____

25–26 that girls sweets

____

27–28 those boys pencils

____

Antony likes outdoor games; he is very popular with the other boys, and he is untidy and noisy. Brian is artistic and he likes making things. He is neat and quiet.

Underline the correct sentences.

29–33 Antony likes playing football.
Brian's books are not very tidy.
Brian likes painting.
Antony is a quiet, tidy boy.
Brian likes craft lessons.
The other boys like Antony.
Antony would rather do woodwork than play cricket.
Brian is often told he must not make so much noise.
Antony would rather play cricket than stay indoors.

5

Copy any **nouns**, **adjectives**, **verbs** and **adverbs** found in the sentence below.

34–40 While walking briskly on a windy Thursday I heard a loud scream.

nouns __________________________________

adjectives __________________________________

verbs __________________________________

adverbs __________________________________

7

A long time ago there lived a poor barber. The barber was poor because
not enough people seemed to want their hair cut or their beards
trimmed. This was the fashion at the time. The barber's wife was always
complaining that she didn't have enough to eat. She would say to her
husband, 'If you did not have enough money to support a wife, why did   5
you marry me? When I was in my father's house I had plenty to eat, but
here there is never anything in the larder.' Then she would take a broom
and beat the poor barber until his back was quite blue.

One day, the barber was so stung by his wife's words – not to mention
the broom – that he decided to leave the house and vowed never to   10
return until he became rich. He packed a bag and set off, trudging the
road from village to village, until he came to the edge of a forest. His feet
ached, so he lay down in the shade of a tall tree to bemoan his hard lot.
'I must be the most unhappy barber in the land,' he moaned, 'perhaps in
the whole world.'   15

As the barber said this, something stirred in the branches of the tree
above him. You see, this tree was the home of a ghost, and ghosts
don't like people coming near their territory. As the ghost floated down,
it spread its long white arms and stood like a tall palm tree before the
barber, its gaping mouth hanging wide open. 'Barber, you must suffer for   20
disturbing me,' cried the ghost. 'I am going to destroy you, you miserable
person.'

The barber had never seen a ghost before, so he behaved as most
people do when they first see one. His legs shook and the hair on his
head stood straight up like the bristles on his wife's broom. But although   25
he was frightened, the barber kept his head. 'Oh, ghostly spirit,' he said
through chattering teeth, 'I wonder whether you will destroy me when I
show you what I have in my bag?'

'Stupid barber,' replied the ghost, 'how can the contents of your bag
prevent me destroying you?' But he was an inquisitive ghost too, and he   *30*
added, 'Let me see what you have in your bag; then I will strike you dead.'
    The barber slowly opened his bag. 'I hardly dare to say this to you,
ghost, but my bag is full of ghosts I have captured during the last few
days. In fact, there is barely room for one more ghost in here before I take
them home for my good wife to make into ghost soup. When I have   *35*
captured you, ghost, and squeezed you into my bag, I'll be on my way.'
So saying, the barber took from his bag the mirror he used to enable his
customers to see whether their beards had been trimmed to their taste.

From *Ghost Soup* by John Paton

Underline the right answers.

1 The barber was unsuccessful because of (his lack of skill, the low
   price for cutting hair, the fashion for longer hair and beards).

2 The barber's wife was angry because (she wanted to stay with her
   father, she did not have enough clothes, she did not have enough to
   eat).

3 The ghost looked like (a black shape, a white sheet, a palm tree).

3

Answer these questions.

4–5 Give two reasons why the barber left home.

(1) ____

(2) ____

6 Why was the ghost angry with the barber?

____

7 Describe what happened to the barber's body when the ghost spoke
   to him.

____

8 What is meant by 'the barber kept his head' in line 26?

____

9 What do you think the barber's plan was?

____

____

6

Underline the **noun** or nouns in each sentence which use the same word in their **plural** and **singular** form.

10 The aircraft flew high in the sky.

11–12 The dressmaker used her scissors to cut the fabric for the clothes.

13 The tourists watched the bison from their coach.

14 The steep Welsh slopes are home to the sheep.

Circle the ous words that have been spelt correctly.

15–20   poisonous   couragous   curious

jealous   hideous   dangeous

serrious   humorous

tremendous

Put a question mark or exclamation mark at the end of each sentence.

21 Catch the thief______

22 Shall we look in this shop______

23 Don't do that______

24 Why does Dad snore so loudly______

25 Can we go swimming now______

26 Hurry up, time is running out______

27 Listen, a siren______

28 Please may I have a sweet______

Circle the words that wouldn't have been widely used a hundred years ago.

29–34 camcorder   DVD player   donkey

cinema   doctor   astronaut   television

candle   microwave   cloth

Put the **pronouns** in the correct columns in the table.

me   yours   hers   I   mine   theirs

35–40

Pronouns about others	Pronouns about myself

6

A witness's report on the robbery

It was about 5.20 pm, though I can't be sure of the exact
time. My watch is a few minutes fast. I was walking down
Nelson Street on my way to the bus stop. There were not many
people around. The shops were getting ready to close and the
streetlights were starting to come on. I was hurrying for the   5
bus but must have missed it, as there was no one waiting at
the stop.

    I just stopped to tie my shoelace up when I saw two men
come by. I looked at them carefully, for some reason. It was
something about the way they behaved. They looked nervous.   10
One of the men was quite tall. He was wearing a raincoat
and blue jeans. I can't remember the colour of his hair but do
remember that he couldn't keep his hands still. He must have
been about 35 or 40. The other man was shorter, and in his
twenties I'd say. He had a blue baseball cap on, with the   15
word 'Italy' written on it. He didn't look very Italian to me, he
was too fair. He was whispering to the tall man, who was still
fidgeting. The men seemed like they were waiting for someone
or something.They were outside Smithards the jewellers. The
lights were still on inside, but I could see the assistants starting   20
to take the rings, brooches and watches out of the window, so
they must have been about to close.

    The men stood there for a moment, looking uncertain what
to do. Then the tall man said 'Now!' He must have said it quite
loudly, because I'm a bit deaf and I definitely heard it.   25

    Immediately the men ran towards the shop and burst through
the door. There was a shout from inside, then some screams. An
alarm started to go off somewhere. It was incredibly loud and
before I knew what was happening I heard police sirens coming
up the street. Just then the men came crashing out of the shop.   30
The tall man in the baseball cap was carrying a bag in his hand.
As they tumbled into the street, they saw the police cars and
just ran for it as fast as they could.

Underline the right answers.

1 The witness was (shopping, coming home from work, going to catch a bus).

2 The two men looked (untidy, nervous, hurried, frightened).

3 It was (daylight, morning, night, twilight).

Answer these questions.

4 What does the taller man do that shows he was nervous?

____

5 How did the witness know the shop was about to close?

____

6–7 List two things that the witness was not sure about.

____

____

8 The witness seems to have made a mistake in describing the men when they came out of the shop. What was it?

____

____

Add the missing commas in each sentence.

9–10 Aman has to buy carrots potatoes rice and tomatoes at the shop.

11–13 At the park Geri Meena David Jason and John all play together.

14–15 On Mark's way to school he passes the police station the swimming pool the park and the shops.

16–17 At the farm the children fed the goats stroked the pigs milked the cows and brushed the horse.

Complete this table of comparing **adjectives**. Some words need their last letter doubled before adding the **suffix**.

18–25

	add 'er'	add 'est'
hot		
tall		
big		
thin		

Complete each word to make a **diminutive**.

ling   let   ock

26 drop______   **27** duck______

28 bull______   **29** book______

Write this sentence again, adding the missing punctuation and capital letters.

30–35 max asked is it time jess got out of bed

____

____

Write *their* or *there* in each of the spaces below. Don't forget to start with a capital letter if necessary.

36 The children went to play with _______________ friends in the swimming pool.

37 _______________ isn't going to be any rain today.

38–39 _______________ shoes are over _______________ on the floor.

40 _______________ was a huge bang as the fireworks exploded.

A Smuggler's Song

If you wake at midnight, and hear a horse's feet
Don't go drawing back the blind, or looking in the street,
Them that asks no questions isn't told a lie.
Watch the wall, my darling, while the Gentlemen go by!
Five and twenty ponies
Trotting through the dark –
Brandy for the Parson,
'Baccy for the Clerk;
Laces for a lady, letters for a spy,
And watch the wall, my darling, while the Gentlemen go by!

Running round the woodlump if you chance to find
Little barrels, roped and tarred, all full of brandy-wine,
Don't you shout to come and look, nor use 'em for your play.
Put the brushwood back again – and they'll be gone next day!
If you see the stable-door setting open wide,
If you see a tired horse lying down inside;
If your mother mends a coat cut about and tore;
If the lining's wet and warm – don't you ask no more!

From *A Smuggler's Song* by Rudyard Kipling

Underline the right answers.

1 Which of these things does the poem tell you to do?

(draw back the blind, look out in the street, ask no questions, shout out if you find barrels)

2 Who are the Gentlemen?

(soldiers, smugglers, rich men, lords)

3 What are the barrels covered with?

(coats, brushwood, straw, grass)

Answer these questions.

4 What time would the smugglers be likely to come?

____

5 What things might the smugglers bring?

____

6 Why does the poem tell you to watch the wall?

____

7 What are the barrels secured with?

____

8 How can you tell this poem is written to a child rather than a grown-up?

____

Add the **suffix** *ship* or *hood* to each of these words.

9 friend_______________

10 neighbour_______________

11 mother_______________

12 apprentice_______________

Add *its* or *it's* to fill the gap in each sentence. Don't forget to start with a capital letter if necessary.

13 _______________ a beautiful day.

14 The cat played with _______________ ball.

15–16 _________________ time you remembered your own bag, _________________ not that hard!

17 Everyone was lined up outside the school; _________________ fire alarm was going.

18 Will's dog lost _________________ ball.

19 _________________ got to be here somewhere!

20 _________________ been a brilliant party. I wish I could have one every week!

Write a **phrase** (group of words) that could describe each of these **nouns**.

Example: bed   _the soft, feathery, comfortable bed_

21 coat ____

22 elephant ____

23 car ____

24 skyscraper ____

25 tree ____

26 egg ____

27 flower ____

Use one of the following **conjunctions** in each gap.

> but   and   so   after   because

28 I missed the train _________________ I overslept.

29 Ahmed is in the cricket team _________________ Josh wasn't good enough.

30 Mum wrapped up my present _________________ I went to bed.

31 Jake bought some toffees _________________ Mike got some too.

32 Cathy's sewing is untidy _________________ she will have to do it again.

33 I like macaroni _________________ my brother likes spaghetti better.

34 The sky was blue _________________ the sun was shining.

Match the words to their **definitions**.

soon   sleepy   error   cautious   herd   adult

35 group of cattle   ________________

36 grown-up   ________________

37 heavy-eyed   ________________

38 careful   ________________

39 mistake   ________________

40 in a short time   ________________   6

Now go to the Progress Chart to record your score!   Total   40

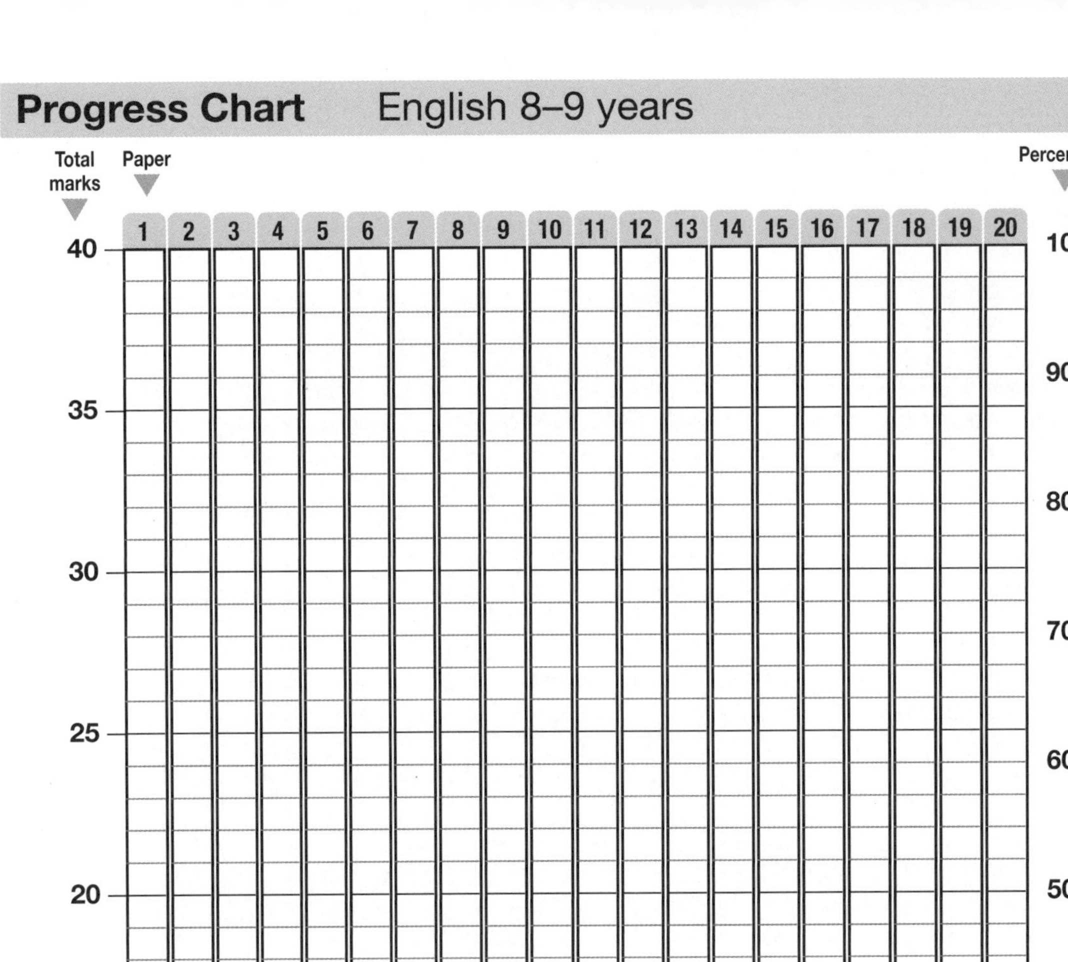

Progress Chart English 8–9 years

When you've finished the book read the Next Steps